C.5

ANNABEL KARMEL

Find out what this is on page 96

DK

DK Publishing

You Can COOK

DK

LONDON, NEW YORK,
MELBOURNE, MUNICH, and DELHI

Designed by Rachael Foster
Edited by Penny Smith,
Lorrie Mack, Wendy Horobin, Fleur Star
Additional design by Rachael Smith,
Lauren Rosier
US editors Liza Kaplan, Margaret Parrish
Photography Dave King
Food stylists Seiko Hatfield,
Martha Dunkerley
Recipe consultant Caroline Stearns
US cooking consultant Wesley Martin

Production editor Sean Daly
Production controller Jen Lockwood
Publishing manager Bridget Giles

First published in the United States in 2010
by DK Publishing, 375 Hudson Street
New York, New York 10014

10 11 12 13 14 10 9 8 7 6 5 4 3 2 1
176543—5/10

Copyright © 2010 Dorling Kindersley Limited

A catalog record for this book is available
from the Library of Congress.

ISBN: 978-0-7566-5863-2

Color reproduction by Alta Images, UK
Printed and bound by Toppan, China

Discover more at
www.dk.com

Contents

About this book

One of the great pleasures in life is eating and if you can cook, you will always be able to conjure up a delicious meal even if you only have a few ingredients.

So I'm going to show you how easy it is to master basic cooking skills, prepare tasty meals, and have fun along the way.

One thing is for sure—everyone loves a good cook!

Bon appetit.

Annabel Karmel

Getting started

Look through this book and choose your recipe. Do you have everything you need? Check, and shop if you are missing anything. Then follow the tips below for safe, hygienic, and happy cooking!

Have fun cooking!

Kitchen safety

☆ Always tie back long hair and roll up loose sleeves so they don't get in the way.

☆ Use oven mitts when handling anything hot.

☆ Keep pan handles turned to the side—you don't want to knock the pans over.

☆ Mop up spills right away so you don't slip on them.

☆ ALWAYS be especially careful when handling sharp knives or electrical equipment.

Kitchen hygiene

☆ The first thing to do when you start cooking is WASH YOUR HANDS!

☆ Cut up meat and vegetables on separate cutting boards.

☆ Wash fruit and vegetables before you cook them.

☆ Store cooked and raw meat in separate compartments in the refrigerator.

☆ Wipe down surfaces and wash dishes when you finish cooking.

Reading the recipes

Symbols to look for

 This tells you how long it takes to prepare a dish. It's just a guide—with practice, you get quicker at cooking.

 This tells you how long a dish takes to cook—on the stove top as well as in the oven.

 This shows the number of servings for older children and adults. Younger children will eat less.

 All the recipes in this book are to be made under adult supervision. But when this symbol appears, extra care should be taken.

Measuring ingredients

Ingredients are measured in cups and spoons, or weighed on scales.

To measure flour
Spoon the flour into a cup and level it off with a knife.

Abbreviations

Metric measures
g = grams
Imperial measures
oz = ounces
lb = pounds

Spoon measures
tsp = teaspoon
tbsp = tablespoon
(Make these level.)

Kitchen equipment

Here's equipment you will find in lots of family kitchens. You'll need to use some of these items to make the recipes in this book.

Icing spatula

Pasta fork

Basting brush

Mallet

Peelers

Sharp knife

Kitchen scissors

Garlic press

Whisks

Wooden spoon

Silicone spatula

Parchment paper

Aluminum foil

Muffin pan

Baking sheet

Round cake pan

Square cake pan

Small bowls

Large bowl

Large saucepan

Crepe pan

Frying pan

Cutting boards

Grater

Electric mixer

Spatulas

Rolling pin

Masher

Strainers

Food blender

Bundt pan

Cooling rack

Small tart pans

Piping bag and tips

Cookie cutters

Wok

Grill pan

Lemon juicer

Colander

Loaf pan

Healthy eating

The key to a healthy diet is to eat lots of different kinds of food. This includes fresh fruit and vegetables, and protein-rich foods to help you grow. Eating cake or cookies as part of this diet is okay, too—just don't eat them all the time, or instead of other foods.

The right stuff
Food is fuel for your body, giving you nutrients (vitamins and minerals) to keep you well. Eating a balanced diet of different kinds of food is all part of being healthy.

33% Carbohydrates

Fruit & vegetables 33%

12% Meat, fish, & protein

Fats & sugar 8%

Milk & dairy 14%

A healthy balance

Every day, you should eat food from all of the five food groups. Each group has a different job to do, but it's important to get the balance right! Fill up on carbohydrates and fruit and vegetables, but don't eat too much fat and sugar.

Carbohydrates
Bread, potatoes, cereals, rice, and pasta give you energy to work and play. Whole-wheat breads and cereals are higher in fiber and give longer lasting energy than white bread or refined cereals.

Fruit and vegetables
You should eat at least five portions of fruit and vegetables every day. Vegetables that are frozen within hours of being picked can be just as nutritious as fresh ones.

Milk and dairy
Dairy foods, such as milk and cheese, contain calcium. Your body needs this mineral to keep your bones, teeth, nails, and hair in good repair. Low-fat and fat-free milk contains as much calcium as whole milk.

Meat, fish, and protein
You need protein to grow. It builds up your muscles and keeps you strong. Protein is found in meat, fish, chicken, eggs, and legumes (peas, beans, nuts, and lentils).

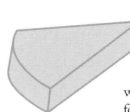

Fats and sugar
Your body needs some fat, but too much can make you sick. Butter, oil, cheese, and food made with these things (such as cake) are fatty. Sugar provides a burst of energy, but too much is bad for your teeth.

Eat a rainbow of color
You can get a good mix of vitamins and minerals by eating a variety of differently colored fruit and vegetables. The more colorful the fruit, the better it is for you, since the color contains antioxidants that help protect us against disease. So a red grapefruit is better for you than an ordinary white grapefruit.

☆ **Annabel's healthy eating tips**
☆Always eat breakfast
☆Eat fruit and or vegetables with every meal
☆If you need a snack, eat fruit rather than sweets
☆Eat fish at least twice a week

Did you know your body is made up of 70% water?

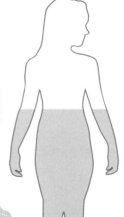

How much should I eat?
Healthy eating is not just about what you eat, but how much, too. If you feel uncomfortably full, you've probably eaten too much! It is a lot more comfortable to eat several smaller meals throughout the day.

Junk food
Food that contains a lot of sugar or fat is called "junk food." It's okay to eat this occasionally, but only as part of a balanced diet. There are some healthier versions in this book that you can make yourself.

Know your fruit

Fruit is not only juicy and scrumptious—it also keeps you healthy and helps you grow strong! Try to eat at least five portions of fruit (or vegetables) every day.

Banana

Apples

Pear

I've used all this lovely fruit in the recipes that follow.

Pineapple

Papaya

Mango

Dried fruit

Dried apricots

Dried cranberries

Raisins

Dried mango

Dried coconut

Golden raisins

Orange

Lemon

Lime

Grapes

Kiwi

Strawberries

Blackberries

Plums

Blueberries

Raspberries

11

Know your vegetables

Most vegetables are bright, crunchy, and full of flavor and they're *very* good for you. Here are the ones you'll use in recipes in this book.

Parsnip

Corn

Potatoes

Onion

Broccoli

Carrots

Red onion

Leek

Garlic

Shallots

Spinach

Zucchini

Iceberg
lettuce

Butternut
squash

Little
gem lettuce

Scallions

Celery

Arugula
leaves

Bell peppers

Tomatoes

Chile
peppers

Green beans

Watercress

Snow peas

Peas

Bean sprouts

Avocado

13

First steps

In this chapter you'll learn the basics of cooking, such as how to make fluffy scrambled eggs or an omelet. And breakfast will never be dull when you can make perfect pancakes or a heart-shaped fried egg in the middle of a slice of toast. You'll find some wonderful, creative ideas for sandwiches and wraps. And for dessert, there are fabulous ways to prepare fruit, from a tropical fruit salad to my indulgent frozen berries with chocolate sauce. So jump in and enjoy the fruits of your labor...

All about EGGS

Eggs are one of the most useful foods we have.

They are fantastic cooked by themselves as a delicious breakfast or light meal, and they are an essential ingredient in lots of recipes, from omelets and pancakes to cookies and cakes. Eggs are packed with protein so they help you grow and stay healthy. Most of the eggs we eat come from chickens.

What's inside an egg?

When you crack open an egg, you'll find the white and the yolk. Although supermarket eggs can't turn into chicks, some other eggs can, and the white and yolk are what the growing chick feeds on.

Brown or white eggs?

You might like one color more than the other, but inside they are just the same. The color comes from the breed of chicken that lays them. Hens that lay brown eggs tend to be bigger than hens that lay white eggs.

Is your egg fresh?

To find out, put it in a bowl of water. If it sinks, it's fresh. But if it floats, it probably isn't—so don't eat it!

Anyone for an egg?

Boiled eggs

The secret to perfect boiled eggs isn't really a secret at all—it's just timing! The longer you cook an egg, the harder it will be.

How do you like your egg?

☆ **Annabel's Tip**
To help stop an egg from cracking when you put it in boiling water, warm it in hot tap water first.

To boil an egg, fill a saucepan with water and bring it to a full boil over high heat.

Lower the egg into the boiling water.

Simmer for **6 minutes** for medium-firm yolks.

A hard-boiled egg...

... takes 12 minutes. When it's done, rop it into cold water to prevent a gray ring from forming around the yolk.

Simmer for **4 minutes** for soft, runny yolks.

Simmer for **8 minutes** for firm yolks.

Scrambled eggs

Cook beaten eggs over low heat and serve them when they're still soft and moist.

Whisk together the eggs, milk, salt, and pepper.

You will need: 2 eggs, 1 tbsp milk, salt and pepper, a pat of butter.

Melt half the butter in a pan. Add the egg mixture and stir constantly while the eggs are cooking. When they start to thicken, stir in the rest of the butter and serve immediately.

Basic omelet

You will need:

2 eggs
salt and pepper
a pat of butter

Here's how you make a delicious basic omelet. Serve it plain, try one of my filling suggestions (below), or invent your own!

Whisk

1 Break the eggs into a bowl and whisk them until they're slightly frothy. Season with salt and pepper.

2 Heat a small frying pan—about 7 in (18 cm)—over medium heat. Melt the butter and when it starts to foam, pour in the eggs.

3 Stir the eggs once or twice, then leave them to cook undisturbed for about 30 seconds.

4 When the eggs start to set at the edge of the pan, lift the cooked edge toward the center. At the same time, tip the pan so the uncooked egg runs into the space that's left. Do this 3 or 4 times until there is no runny egg left on the surface of the omelet.

Lift

Omelet fillings

• small handful of ham, cut into strips, with slices of tomato

• ¼ cup grated hard cheese such as Cheddar or Gruyère

• 1 slice (approximately 1 oz/30 g) smoked salmon, cut into thin strips

• 1 tsp chopped soft herbs—try parsley with dill, chervil, or chives

• 1 tbsp each of corn and diced red bell pepper, plus one thinly sliced scallion

• handful of white button mushrooms sautéed in a pat of butter

Fold

5 Now add your filling. Here, we're using a handful of fresh parsley, sprinkled all over the eggs. Or, if you like, whisk your herbs into the eggs at step 1.

6 Turn off the heat and fold the omelet over. Transfer it to a plate and serve immediately.

Eat up while it's still hot!

How to make toast

It's easy to make toast in a toaster, but it tastes just as nice when you use a broiler. Lay your bread on the broiler pan, then put it close to the heat—it takes only a couple of minutes for one side to turn golden. When it does, turn the bread over and toast the other side.

☆Annabel's Tip

Once the toast is made, let it stand for a minute or two. This lets the steam escape so the toast doesn't get soggy.

Now you can treat yourself to my tasty toast toppers

Tomato and cheese

You will need: butter, 1 slice toast, 1 sliced tomato, pepper, ⅓ cup grated hard cheese such as Cheddar

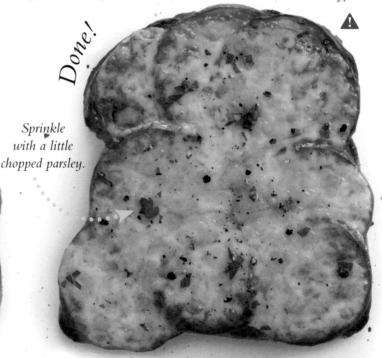

Ready to broil

Done!

Sprinkle with a little chopped parsley.

1 Heat the broiler to high. Spread a little butter on the toast and lay thin slices of tomato on it. Let the tomato overhang the crust to keep the crust from burning. Season with pepper, then scatter cheese over the top.

2 Broil for 1½ to 2 minutes until the cheese is bubbling and turning brown. It will be hot! So let it cool a little before you eat it.

Hearty egg

You will need: 2 tsp oil, 1 lightly toasted slice of bread, 1 egg, salt and pepper

You can eat this piece, too!

Use a cookie cutter to make a hole in your toast.

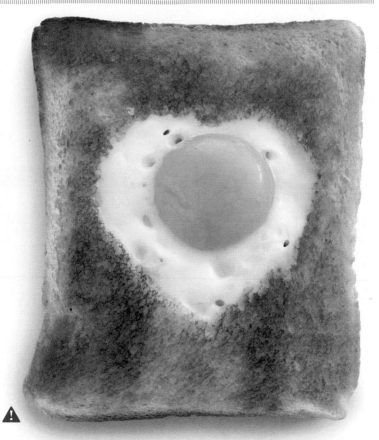

Heat the oil in a small frying pan. Cut a hole in the middle of the toast. Break the egg into a cup. Put the toast in the frying pan and gently slide the egg into the hole. Add a little salt and pepper. Turn the heat to low and cook for about 4 minutes until the egg white has set. Then serve. ⚠

Here are some savory "toasties"—sweet ones are on the next page

Grilled garlic toast

You will need: 2 tbsp softened butter, 1 small clove crushed garlic, 2 tbsp grated Parmesan cheese, pepper, 4 slices toasted French bread

1 Heat the broiler to high. Mix together the butter, garlic, Parmesan, and freshly ground pepper. Spread the butter mixture generously on the toast.

Sprinkle with chopped parsley

2 Broil for about 30 seconds until melted. Sprinkle with parsley and ⚠ serve immediately.

21

Caramelized bananas

You will need: butter, 1 slice toast, 1 sliced banana, ½ tbsp light brown sugar, pinch of cinnamon

1 Preheat the broiler to high. Lightly butter the toast and lay the banana on top. Mix together the sugar and cinnamon and sprinkle over the banana.

2 Broil for 1 or 2 minutes until the sugar is bubbling and golden. Watch carefully so it doesn't burn. Cool slightly before serving. ⚠

Try some sweet toppings on your toast, too. Fruit is perfect!

Broiled peaches and honey

You will need: butter, 1 slice toast, 1 sliced peach, 1 tbsp mascarpone cheese, 1 tsp honey

For bread try brioche or challah

Serve while still warm

1 Preheat the broiler to medium. Lightly butter the toast and lay the peach slices on top.

2 Broil gently until the peaches soften, then add the mascarpone cheese and drizzle the honey over the top.

⚠ 22

Real hot chocolate

Once you've had hot chocolate made with *real* chocolate you'll never want any other kind!

You will need:

1 cup milk
1 oz (30 g) chopped dark chocolate
¼ tsp vanilla extract
2 tsp sugar (or to taste)

☆ **Annabel's Tip**

For even more of a treat, top your hot chocolate with whipped cream, a dusting of cocoa, or a sprinkling of shaved chocolate.

Try it with milk chocolate instead

Frothy top

1 Put the milk in a pan and gently bring it to a boil.

2 Put the chocolate, vanilla, and sugar into a heat-proof pitcher.

3 Pour the hot milk onto the chocolate and whisk until the chocolate has melted. Serve while it's still frothy on top.

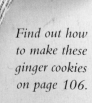

Find out how to make these ginger cookies on page 106.

23

Crepes

These tasty crepes are easier to make than you'd think. The first one you make may be a bit messy, since the pan's still warming up—think of it as the cook's treat!

You will need:

1 cup all-purpose flour
pinch of salt
1 egg
1¼ cups milk
1 tbsp butter, melted
canola oil, for greasing

1 Put the flour and salt in a large bowl. Make a well in the center, then add the egg and half the milk.

2 Whisk into a thick, smooth batter. Then whisk in the rest of the milk and melted butter. Or just mix everything in a blender.

3 Heat a small nonstick frying pan—about 8 in (20 cm)—over medium heat. Grease the pan with oil. Pour in 3 tbsp batter. Tilt the pan so the batter covers the base.

4 Cook for 1 to 1½ minutes until golden brown underneath. Then flip the crepe with a spatula (or toss it if you dare!) and cook for another minute.

Serve with sugar and lemon

☆Annabel's Tip
To serve the crepes all at once, stack them on a plate with baking parchment in between each one and keep them warm in a low oven.

Pancakes

Pancakes are a great way to start the day, since they give you lots of energy. Since these are quite small, you should be able to cook two or three at one time.

You will need:

1⅓ cups all-purpose flour
2 tbsp sugar
½ tsp baking soda
1 tsp baking powder
large pinch of salt
1 cup buttermilk
1 egg
¼ tsp vanilla extract
1½ cups blueberries
canola oil, for greasing
2 tbsp maple syrup

1 Put the flour, sugar, baking soda, baking powder, and salt in a bowl. Add half the buttermilk, the egg, and vanilla extract.

2 Whisk everything together to make a batter. Add the remaining buttermilk and whisk until smooth.

3 Add the blueberries and gently mix them into the batter. Try not to squash them.

4 Lightly oil and heat a nonstick frying pan over medium heat. Drop in 2 tbsp batter per pancake. Cook for 1½ to 2 minutes until golden underneath and bubbling on top. Flip over and cook for another 1 to 2 minutes. Serve with maple syrup.

For extra flavor, serve with a pat of butter

☆Annabel's Tip

You don't have to use buttermilk in this recipe. Instead, mix together ½ cup plain yogurt and ½ cup fat-free milk.

All sorts of sandwiches

A sandwich is just two slices of bread with filling inside. But there are zillions of variations—different fillings... different breads... toasted or plain... Here are a few ideas.

First, choose your bread

Spread mayonnaise on a slice of toast. Add a layer of cranberry sauce.

Chicken club sandwich

To prepare your ingredients, toast 3 slices of bread, slice a small, cooked, skinless chicken breast, broil 2 strips bacon until crisp, slice 1 tomato, and shred 2 lettuce leaves. Then follow the steps (right) to put the sandwich together.

Add half the sliced, cooked chicken and scatter half the crispy bacon over the top.

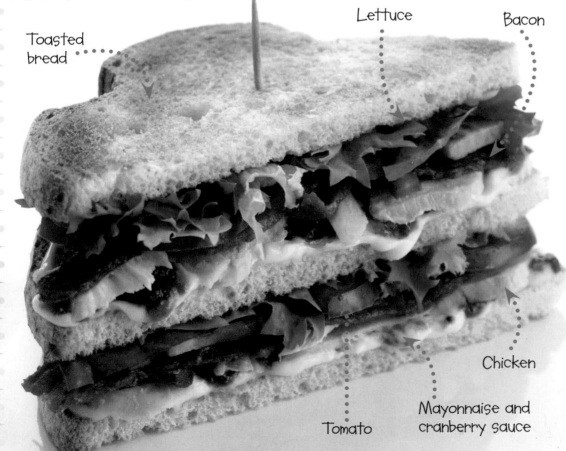

Toasted bread

Lettuce

Bacon

Chicken

Mayonnaise and cranberry sauce

Tomato

Add half the sliced tomato and shredded lettuce, and add salt and pepper.

Put another layer of toast on top. Then repeat the steps above.

Ham with honey-mustard mayonnaise

Tomato

Seeded roll

Sliced ham

Lettuce

Mayonnaise

1 To make the mustard mayonnaise, mix together 1 tbsp mayonnaise, ¼ tsp whole-grain mustard, and ¼ tsp honey.

2 Spread the mustard mixture on a bread roll. Put a slice of ham on top, followed by slices of tomato and a couple of lettuce leaves. Put the top on the roll and serve immediately.

Ricotta and roasted vegetables

Ciabatta bread

Torn basil

Red onion

Bell pepper

Ricotta cheese

Zucchini

1 To roast the vegetables, put slices of red onion, zucchini, and red and yellow bell peppers on a baking sheet. Drizzle with olive oil and roast at 400°F (200°C) for 20 minutes.

2 Spread a layer of ricotta cheese over a slice of ciabatta bread. Scatter on the roasted vegetables and a few torn basil leaves. Season with pepper and serve.

27

Open-faced sandwiches

Egg, cheese, and chive

Sprouts

Hard-boiled egg

Baguette

Yogurt and chive dressing

Grated cheese

To make the yogurt dressing, mix together 1 tbsp Greek yogurt, 1 tbsp mayonnaise, ½ tsp lemon juice, and 1 tsp snipped chives. Spread the mixture over the baguette. Then add grated Cheddar cheese, sliced hard-boiled egg, and sprouts.

Shrimp and watercress

Watercress

Shrimp
Use either fresh or thawed frozen shrimp in this sandwich. Drain the shrimp first on paper towels.

Shrimp in dressing

Slice of lemon

Ciabatta

To make the dressing, mix together 1 tsp mayonnaise, ¾ tsp lemon juice, salt, and pepper. Gently stir in 3 oz (85 g) cooked shrimp. Lightly butter the ciabatta (or use a baguette). Put a handful of watercress on top, then the dressed shrimp. Garnish with lemon.

Wraps

Tomato, mozzarella, and pesto

⚠️ Warm the tortilla in a dry frying pan. Spread over the pesto and mayonnaise mixture, then lay the mozzarella and tomato down the center of the tortilla. Season with salt and pepper and roll up.

☆ **Annabel's Tip**
To make your wraps easier to serve, fasten them closed with a toothpick.

Flour tortilla (about 7 in/18 cm)

1 tbsp mayonnaise mixed with 1 tsp pesto

1 large tomato, skinned, seeded, and quartered

2 oz (60 g) sliced mozzarella

Chicken wrap

⚠️ Warm the tortilla in a dry frying pan. Mix the mayonnaise with 2 to 3 drops of lemon juice and ½ tbsp ketchup (or just squirt the ketchup onto the tortilla) and spread over the tortilla. Then scatter lettuce over half the tortilla and layer the chicken and tomatoes on top. Add salt and pepper and roll up.

Shredded lettuce

Flour tortilla (about 7 in/18 cm)

1 oz (30 g) cooked chicken

1 tbsp mayonnaise

3 cherry tomatoes

Lemon

Roll up and eat!

½ tbsp ketchup

29

Cooking vegetables

Vegetables are a great way to add color, texture, and healthy vitamins to a meal. Roast, boil, steam, or stir-fry your favorites.

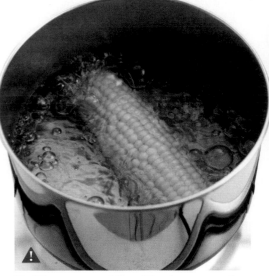

Steam

Boiling vegetables Use just enough water (slightly salted) to cover the vegetables. Bring to a boil, add the vegetables, and cook until just soft but still a bit firm.

Steaming vegetables Cover the bottom of a pan with water. Add a steamer basket and bring the water to a boil. Then add your vegetables and put the lid on the pan. The vegetables hold on to most of their nutrients as they cook in the steam.

Roasted parsnip chips

2 Line a baking sheet with baking parchment. Lay the sliced parsnips on this. Sprinkle with olive oil and season with salt and pepper.

Roast

1 Preheat the oven to 350°F (180°C). Peel 2 parsnips and cut off the ends. Then cut the parsnips into thin slices—make them all about the same size.

Stir-fried vegetables with...   ... sweet chili

For the sauce
1½ tbsp soy sauce
1 to 2 tsp sweet chili sauce
(or to taste)

You will need:

3 oz (85 g) snow peas, trimmed
1 large carrot
½ red bell pepper, seeded
3 oz (85 g) broccoli
1 tbsp canola oil
½ tsp grated peeled fresh ginger
2 oz (60 g) bean sprouts
2 scallions, thinly sliced

1 Cut the snow peas, carrot, and pepper into matchstick-sized pieces. Cut the broccoli into bite-sized florets.

2 Heat the oil in a wok or large frying pan over a high heat. Add the ginger and let it sizzle for 10 seconds, then add the carrots, pepper, and broccoli and stir-fry for 2 minutes.

3 Add the bean sprouts and snow peas and stir-fry for one minute. Stir in the scallions, then remove from the heat, and stir in the soy sauce and the sweet chili sauce. Serve immediately.

3 Roast for 15 minutes. Then turn the slices over and roast for 10 minutes. Turn them again and roast for a final 5 to 10 minutes until golden.

Fruit, glorious fruit!

There are lots of yummy ways to eat fruit, whether it's fresh, frozen, or cooked.

Tropical fruit salad

You will need:

For the sauce
1 small ripe mango
3 tbsp tropical fruit juice
1 tbsp lime juice
1 tbsp confectioner's sugar

For the salad
½ fresh pineapple
2 oranges
1 papaya
2 small bananas

1 To make the sauce, peel and slice the mango. Push it through a strainer, then mix it with the tropical fruit juice, lime juice, and sugar. Or simply whizz the sauce ingredients together in a blender.

2 For the salad, peel and core the pineapple. Cut the fruit into cubes.

3 Peel the oranges and cut into segments. Cube the papaya, then peel and slice the bananas. Mix the fruit and add the sauce.

Serve with a candied cherry

32

Frozen berries

You will need:

10 oz (300 g) fresh berries
(such as blackberries, raspberries,
blueberries, and strawberries)
4 oz (110 g) white chocolate,
chopped into small pieces
⅔ cup heavy cream

1 Freeze the berries on a baking sheet
lined with parchment. Divide them
between 4 bowls. Let them thaw slightly.

2 Put the white chocolate into a bowl.
Warm the cream until it is hot but
not boiling. Pour the hot cream over
the white chocolate and stir until melted.

Pour the sauce on top and serve immediately

Pear and plum crumble

Make six little crumbles or one big one

You will need:

1 lb (450 g) pears, cored and cut into
chunks
1 lb (450 g) plums, pitted and quartered
¼ cup superfine sugar

For the crumble topping
1 cup all-purpose flour
½ cup whole-wheat flour
½ tsp salt
¾ stick butter
½ cup rolled oats
1 tsp ground ginger
½ cup turbino sugar

1 Preheat the oven to 400°F (200°C).
Put the pears and plums into six
heat-proof dishes. Sprinkle the sugar
over the top.

2 Put the flour and salt in a bowl. Rub in
the butter. Then stir in the oats, ginger,
and sugar. Sprinkle the topping on the fruit.
Cook small crumbles for 30 minutes, and
one large one for 40 to 45 minutes.

☆ **Annabel's Tip**
*The crumble is cooked when it's golden
on top and bubbling at the sides.*

Light bites

When you're feeling a bit hungry it's good to have healthy foods on hand. Try making delicious soup like my corn chowder, fill baked potatoes with tempting toppings, or design your own fabulous fruit smoothies. And there are delicious salads here, too. Not only will they make a tasty light meal—they are also a nice change from sandwiches in your lunchbox...

Corn chowder

A chowder is a lusciously thick and warming soup, usually made with potato. Use this recipe to make either a vegetarian or a chicken version.

You will need:

1 medium onion
1 small clove garlic
2 medium potatoes
1 tbsp butter
3 cups vegetable broth
½ cup milk
1 x 7 oz (200 g) can corn, drained
⅓ cup heavy cream

1 Chop the onion finely, crush the garlic, and peel and cut the potatoes into small cubes.

2 Melt the butter in a large saucepan. Cook the onion and garlic very gently for 10 to 12 minutes, until soft.

3 Add the potato cubes, broth, and milk. Bring the mixture to a boil, then reduce the heat and simmer, partly covered, for 15 minutes.

4 Add the corn and simmer (again, partly covered) for 5 to 10 minutes more, until the potato is soft. If the mixture feels very thick, add 2 to 3 tbsp hot water.

Chicken chowder

To make this version, use chicken broth and add 1 cup shredded, cooked chicken when you get to step 6.

5 Turn off the heat. Leave the mixture to cool, then put half aside in a bowl. If you have a hand blender, blend the remaining half in the saucepan until smooth. (Otherwise, puree it in a blender and return it to the saucepan.)

6 Add the soup in the bowl to the soup in the saucepan and stir in the cream. Reheat gently to serve.

Sprinkle dill on top for flavor and color

☆ **Annabel's Tip**
Chowder is usually served with crumbled crackers such as saltines or oyster crackers—or try delicious crusty bread (see page 44).

You will need:

2 small boneless chicken breasts
2 red bell peppers
5 oz (140 g) fusilli pasta
olive oil, to brush the grill pan
3 to 4 handfuls arugula

For the marinade

2 tbsp olive oil
2 tsp lemon juice
1 clove garlic, crushed
salt and pepper
2 sprigs fresh thyme

For the dressing

¼ cup light olive oil
3 tbsp rice-wine vinegar
1½ tsp Dijon mustard
1 tbsp green pesto
2 tbsp snipped chives
2 tbsp chopped parsley

Chicken pasta salad with roasted peppers

To make this dish, you bash chicken with a mallet, peel bell peppers, and mix up a herb dressing. I've cooked my chicken on a grill pan to make it striped, but an ordinary frying pan is fine.

Lemony marinated chicken

Sweet roasted bell peppers

Time saver
Marinating the chicken gives it a fresh lemony flavor. But if you don't have time, you can leave out this step. The dish isn't the same, but it's still very tasty!

Bash

1 Preheat the oven to 400°F (200°C). Cover the chicken with plastic wrap. Then bash it a few times with a mallet to flatten it.

Marinate

2 For the marinade, mix up the oil, lemon juice, garlic, salt and pepper, and thyme sprigs. Pour it over the chicken and leave for at least 20 minutes.

3 Cut the bell peppers in half and take out the seeds and pith. Roast the bell peppers in the oven for 20 minutes, until soft with blackened skins.

4 Put the bell peppers in a bowl. Cover with plastic wrap and leave to cool. Peel off the skins and slice the flesh into thin strips.

5 Cook the pasta in boiling water following the package instructions. Drain, then rinse the pasta in cold water.

6 To cook the chicken, brush a grill pan or frying pan with a little oil and heat it up. Cook the chicken for 4 minutes on each side or until done.

7 To make the dressing, mix together the oil, vinegar, mustard, pesto, chives, and parsley.

8 When the chicken is cool enough to handle, cut it into bite-sized strips.

Mix

9 Put the chicken in a bowl with the bell peppers, pasta, and arugula. Add the dressing and mix everything together with your (very clean) hands. Serve.

Cobb salad

You will need:

- 2 eggs
- 2 oz (60 g) Cheddar cheese
- 2 oz (60 g) skinless, cooked chicken breast
- 1 large tomato
- 1 small avocado
- 1 small little gem lettuce or ½ heart of romaine lettuce
- 3 tbsp mayonnaise
- 2 tbsp milk
- ½ tsp red-wine vinegar
- ¼ tsp Dijon mustard
- 2 to 3 drops Worcestershire sauce
- salt and pepper

This popular main course salad is made with avocado, hard-boiled eggs, and chicken. Serve it with fresh crusty bread for supper.

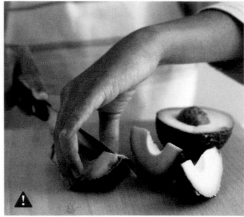

1 Bring a saucepan of water to a boil. Lower the eggs into the water and simmer for 12 minutes.

2 Transfer the eggs to a bowl of ice water (or run cold water over them). When cool, peel off the shells. Cut each egg into 4 lengthwise. Dice the cheese and chicken into very small cubes. Cut the tomato into eight pieces.

3 Slice the avocado and remove the skin. Then arrange the lettuce, avocado, egg, tomato, chicken, and cheese in a bowl.

Make the dressing

For the dressing, whisk together the mayonnaise, milk, vinegar, mustard, Worcestershire sauce, salt, and pepper and serve with the salad.

Sprinkle with parsley

40

Layered salad

This colorful striped salad looks fantastic turned out like a gelatin mold.

You will need:

4 oz (110 g) small pasta shells
¼ cup light mayonnaise
3 tbsp low-fat sour cream
2 tbsp ketchup
2 tsp lemon juice
8 oz (250 g) salad-size cooked shrimp, drained and dried
2 tbsp chopped parsley
salt and pepper
1 x 7 oz (198 g) can corn, drained
1 large carrot, peeled and grated
1 bunch scallions, finely sliced
¼ head iceberg lettuce, thinly sliced

1 Cook the pasta following the package instructions, then drain. Cool under cold running water. In a bowl, mix together the mayonnaise, sour cream, ketchup, lemon juice, shrimp, parsley, and salt and pepper.

2 Line a 1 quart (1 liter) bowl with plastic wrap. Spoon half of the shrimp mixture into the base. Put the pasta on top. Then sprinkle on the drained corn. Lay the grated carrot on this. Then add the remaining shrimp, scallions, and lettuce. Press down firmly. Chill in the refrigerator for 1 hour.

3 Just before serving, put the salad into the freezer for 10 minutes. Then place a plate on top of the salad. Hold tightly, and turn the bowl and plate over to turn out the salad.

Flip over to turn out

Half the shrimp

Pasta

Corn

Carrot

Half the shrimp

Scallions and lettuce

Add a twist of lemon and sprig of parsley

41

Making bread dough

It only takes a little effort and a few simple ingredients to make bread dough that's perfect for delicious small loaves, rolls, speciality breads—and pizza!

1 Put ¼ cup of the warm (hand-hot) water in a small bowl with the sugar. Stir in the yeast and leave to stand for 10 minutes.

The yeast should start to froth. Frothy yeast looks like this.

2 Stir together the salt and flour in a large bowl. Make a well in the center and pour in the melted butter and frothing yeast.

6 Transfer to a lightly oiled bowl, cover with plastic wrap, and leave in a warm place for 1 hour to prove (double in size).

When the dough has doubled in size, it looks like this.

7 Punch down the dough—this means using your fists to squash out the air, then kneading it some more.

You will need:

1¼ cups warm water
1 tbsp sugar
1 x ¼ oz (7 g) package dried yeast
1 tsp salt

3½ cups white bread
flour, plus extra for dusting
1 tbsp melted butter
sunflower or canola oil, for greasing
1 egg, beaten

Kneaded enough?
Poke a finger into
the dough—if
it's ready, it
will spring
back.

3 Rinse out the yeast bowl with
¾ cup of the water and add to
the flour. Mix to make a soft dough,
adding more water as needed.

4 In the bowl, start forming the
dough into a ball shape, ready to
knead. Dust your work surface with
flour to stop the dough from sticking.

5 Knead the dough for 10 minutes—
use the heel of your hand to push it
down and away from you. Fold over
the top end, turn it, and repeat.

8 We wanted to make 2 small
loaves, so we divided the dough
into 2 pieces. (See the next page for
lots of other ideas.)

9 Put each piece in a greased
1 lb (450 g) loaf pan. Cover
with oiled plastic wrap and leave to
prove again—for about 20 minutes
this time, or until doubled in size.

10 While the bread is proving,
preheat the oven to 400°F (200°C).
Brush the loaves with beaten egg. Bake
for 25 to 35 minutes, until golden on top
and hollow-sounding underneath.

What to make with your dough

To make bread rolls

Divide the dough in half, then half again, and keep going until you have 16 pieces. Make into round shapes, then put on greased or lined baking sheets. Cover with oiled plastic wrap and leave to prove in a warm place for 20 minutes, or until doubled in size. Brush with beaten egg and decorate with seeds. Then bake in the oven for 15 to 20 minutes.

2 cottage loaves...

...or 16 small rolls

To decorate bread rolls

Plain rolls are delicious, but it's fun choosing different toppings, too. Try grated Parmesan cheese or sunflower, poppy, and sesame seeds.

Cottage loaves

Divide the dough equally into two. Then divide each piece into two again, but this time make one piece twice as big as the other. Shape the pieces into rounds. Put the large rounds on an oiled baking sheet, with the small rounds on top. Push the floured handle of a wooden spoon through the middle of each loaf to join the two parts together. Brush the tops with beaten egg before baking.

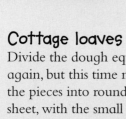

... or 2 small loaves...

Freezing bread

After the first prove, punch down the dough and shape it into rolls. Freeze on a baking sheet lined with plastic wrap. Then transfer to resealable bags and store in the freezer. Leave in a warm place to defrost and prove, then cook as before.

Is it ready?

The bread will be golden brown when it's done. And when you tap the base with your hand, it will sound hollow.

... or 2 pieces of focaccia

Focaccia

Shape your dough into two flatish rectangles and leave to prove for 20 minutes. Brush with olive oil and sprinkle with sea salt. Then poke in pieces of rosemary. Cook the focaccia for 20 minutes or until golden on top with a hollow-sounding base.

Perfect baked potatoes

Baked potatoes are the easiest meal ever—just put them in the oven and leave them to cook. All the recipes here are for four medium potatoes.

1 Preheat the oven to 400°F (200°C). Wash and dry the potatoes and rub oil all over their skins. Prick them with a fork so the moisture inside can escape as steam during cooking.

2 Put the potatoes on a baking sheet and bake them for 1 to 1½ hours. They are ready when the skins are crisp and the flesh is soft inside (push a fork in to check).

Cut a cross in the top of each potato and serve with butter and a little salt…

… or try my tasty filling ideas

Melting butter

☆**Annabel's Tip**
Choose potatoes that are firm and heavy. Cut out any blemishes or green parts before you cook them.

Cheese and squash filling

Peel, seed, and slice ½ large butternut squash. Bake for 40 minutes with the potato. Scoop out the cooked potato and squash and mash together with 1½ cups grated Cheddar cheese, ½ cup crème fraiche or sour cream, salt, and pepper. Put back into the skins.

Tuna topping

Mix one 6 oz (185 g) can drained tuna with 2 sliced scallions, ¼ cup crème fraiche or sour cream, 1 tbsp milk, 1 tsp lemon juice, 4 drops Worcestershire sauce, and ¼ cup corn. Spoon onto 4 potatoes and top with 1 cup grated Cheddar cheese.

Sprinkle with Parmesan cheese…

…and bake for another 15 minutes

Broil until golden, then serve

Crispy bacon potatoes

Broil 8 strips of bacon until crisp. Blot on paper towels. Scoop out the cooked potato and mash with ½ cup sour cream, 2 tbsp butter, and 2 tbsp milk. Stir in 1 tsp snipped chives, salt, and pepper. Spoon back into the potato skins and crumble the bacon over the top.

Crispy bacon

Snipped chives

Heat through in the oven before serving

47

Quick dips

Raspberry sauce

Whizz two handfuls of raspberries and a teaspoon of raspberry jam in a blender. Strain to remove seeds.

Dip pear and mango in the sauce ⚠

Guacamole and tomato salsa

For the guacamole mash an avocado with the juice of ½ a lime, 1 tbsp of Greek yogurt, salt, and pepper. Stir in your choice of a finely chopped scallion, a chopped tomato, or 1 to 2 tsp of chopped cilantro.

Serve with tortilla chips or vegetable sticks ⚠

For the tomato salsa put 2 halved tomatoes in a food processor with 4 chopped scallions, ¼ seeded red bell pepper, ¼ seeded red chile, salt, and pepper. Pulse until coarsely chopped.

Cottage-cheese dip

Chill and serve with fresh vegetables

Whizz 1 cup cottage cheese with 3 tbsp mayonnaise, 2 tbsp ketchup, ¼ tsp lemon juice, 3 drops Worcestershire sauce. ⚠

48

Yogurt dip with caramel sauce

Dip in your favorite fruit

Swirl a teaspoon of caramel sauce through a big dollop of Greek yogurt and serve with pieces of fresh fruit.

Perfect popcorn

Warm, freshly popped corn is a delicious treat tossed in a little melted butter and a sprinkling of salt. Or try my special sweet variation.

You will need:

1 tbsp sunflower oil
½ cup popping corn

1 Heat the oil in a large heavy-bottomed pan. When the oil is shimmering, add the corn. Put on the lid.

2 Let the corn pop for a minute or two until the popping starts to subside. Then shake the pan and let the corn pop again. Repeat until all the corn has popped.

Popcorn crunch

Melt ½ stick butter, ½ cup light brown sugar, 2 tbsp maple syrup or golden syrup, and a pinch of salt in a pan. Mix with your cooked popcorn. Spread out on a baking sheet and bake for 25 to 30 minutes at 300°F (150°C). Stir halfway through. Cool before eating.

Popped and ready to eat

Unpopped kernels

49

Fruit smoothies

Good colors, good flavors, good for you!
And these smoothies are so easy to make—
all you do is whizz up a few ingredients.
For extra-thick smoothies, use frozen fruit.

Put your ingredients in a blender,
put on the lid, press the button,
and whizz!

Make your own delicious drinks

Blackberry and blueberry

You will need:

½ cup blackberries
½ cup sliced strawberries
½ cup blueberries
¼ banana
¼ cup blueberry yogurt
2 tsp honey

Put the berries and banana in a blender with the yogurt and honey. Blend until all the lumps have gone and it's a pretty deep purple color.

Pineapple, mango, and banana

You will need:

1 small ripe mango (peeled and pitted)
¼ banana
¼ cup canned pineapple chunks
plus ⅓ cup of the juice
¼ cup vanilla yogurt

Put the mango, banana, pineapple plus juice, and yogurt into a blender and whizz until smooth.

Banana caramel

You will need:

2½ tbsp caramel sauce
½ cup milk
1 large banana
¼ cup Greek yogurt

Put 1 tsp of the caramel into a small bowl and mix with 1 tsp of the milk. Set aside while you make the smoothie.

Put the remaining caramel, banana, and yogurt in a blender and whizz it all together. Add the rest of the milk and whizz again. Drizzle over the thinned caramel before serving.

Double strawberry

You will need:

1 cup sliced strawberries
¼ banana
⅓ cup strawberry yogurt
2 tsp honey

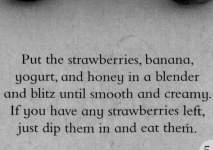

Put the strawberries, banana, yogurt, and honey in a blender and blitz until smooth and creamy. If you have any strawberries left, just dip them in and eat them.

Main meals

Here I show you how to make some of my favorite recipes, whether it's healthy fast food, such as my yummy burgers, or fantastic new flavors such as those in my spicy chicken. Making your own pasta is fun, too. And there's nothing quite as delicious as fresh pasta with my quick-and-easy pesto sauce or hidden-vegetable tomato sauce. Give Mom and Dad the night off and conjure up some specials in the kitchen…

Sticky chicken drumsticks

You will need:

4 chicken drumsticks
pepper

For the marinade
1 tsp balsamic vinegar
2 tbsp soy sauce
2 tbsp honey
1 small garlic clove
½ tsp grated fresh ginger

To pack this dish with flavor and make it gorgeously sticky, soak the drumsticks in spicy-sweet marinade before cooking. This works the flavors into the meat and adds a lovely glaze.

Cook until golden brown

☆ Annabel's Tip

If you are short of bowls, try marinating the chicken in a small plastic food bag.

Making the marinade

Marinating the chicken adds flavor and makes it tender. Sometimes you need to marinate the meat overnight, but this recipe takes only 20 minutes.

1 First, put the balsamic vinegar, soy sauce, and honey in a bowl.

fresh ginger

garlic

Crush

soy sauce

balsamic vinegar

honey

2 Remove the papery skin from a clove of garlic and put the garlic in a garlic press. Squeeze it into the bowl.

3 Peel a piece of fresh ginger and grate it on a fine grater. It's easier if you freeze the ginger first. Take care not to scrape your fingers on the blade.

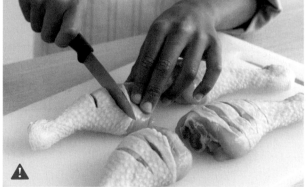

Pour

1 Slash the drumsticks with a sharp knife and season with freshly ground black pepper. Put the drumsticks in an oven-proof dish, then pour over the marinade so it coats the chicken. Put the chicken in the fridge for 20 minutes.

2 Preheat the oven to 400°F (200°C). Bake the drumsticks in the marinade for 45 minutes or until cooked through, turning and basting every 10 minutes or so.

You will need:

½ cup fresh white bread crumbs
1 tbsp Parmesan cheese, grated
1 tbsp chopped parsley
2 skinless, boneless chicken breast fillets
salt and pepper
1 egg, beaten
canola oil, for frying

Chicken scallops

Eat this dish straight from the pan while the coating is still tasty and crisp. The scallops are made from flattened chicken breasts, so they cook in just a few minutes.

Or try...
... this recipe with pork fillet or medallions instead of chicken. Just give the pork an extra minute or two to cook, and serve with fresh vegetables.

Serve with small new potatoes and fresh green beans

A light coating of bread crumbs makes it nice and crunchy

1 For the bread crumbs, whizz together 2 or 3 slices of white bread. Add the Parmesan and parsley.

2 Cover the chicken breasts with plastic wrap and bash them with a mallet until they are very thin.

3 Season the chicken with salt and pepper and dip in the beaten egg.

4 Coat the chicken in the bread crumb mixture.

5 Heat the oil in a large frying pan. Fry the chicken on medium heat for about 3 minutes on each side until golden and cooked through.

Tomato sauce with spaghetti

You will need:

1 tbsp sunflower oil
1 onion, chopped
1 clove garlic, crushed
1 x 14 oz (400 g) can diced tomatoes
1½ tbsp tomato paste
½ tsp sugar
1 tsp fresh thyme
1 tbsp chopped fresh basil
6 oz (170 g) dried spaghetti

1 Heat the oil in a pan. Add the onion and garlic and sauté for 2 to 3 minutes. Add the diced tomatoes and tomato paste, sugar, thyme, and basil. Bring to a boil, cover, and simmer for 20 minutes. Serve, or for a smoother sauce, whizz to a puree in a blender.

2 Cook the spaghetti following the package instructions. Drain and serve with the sauce.

Perfect with the chicken!

These ingredients give the tikka its distinctive flavor

root ginger

ground coriander

garlic

garam masala

mild curry powder

Spicy chicken

This delicious supper is based on an Indian dish called chicken tikka masala. Serve it with basmati rice and pappadams.

Marinate

You will need:

2 boneless, skinless chicken breast fillets, cubed
salt and pepper

For the marinade

⅓ cup yogurt
½ tsp grated fresh ginger
1 small clove garlic, crushed
½ tsp mild curry powder

For the sauce

1 tbsp butter
1 medium onion, chopped
1 tsp garam masala
¼ tsp ground coriander
¼ tsp freshly grated ginger
1 cup chicken broth
1 tbsp honey
1 tbsp tomato paste
1 x 14 oz (400 g) can diced tomatoes
⅔ cup heavy cream
1 tbsp lemon juice

1 For the marinade, mix together the yogurt, ginger, garlic, and curry powder. Add the chicken and mix to coat. Cover and put in the fridge for 2 hours or overnight.

Sauté

2 To make the sauce, melt the butter over medium heat and sauté the onion for 5 minutes. Add the garam masala, ground coriander, and ginger and sauté for another 5 minutes.

3 Add the broth, honey, tomato paste, and canned tomatoes. Stir, then simmer for 15 minutes.

Simmer

4 Add the cream and simmer for 10 more minutes until thick.

5 Line a baking sheet with aluminium foil and arrange the marinated chicken cubes on it. Broil for 8 to 10 minutes, turning the pieces over halfway through cooking.

6 Add the cooked chicken and lemon juice to the sauce. Season to taste with salt and pepper. Simmer for a couple of minutes, then serve with fluffy boiled rice.

Spicy tips
Store your spices in airtight jars away from bright sunlight. And don't keep them when they're past their sell-by date, since they will probably have lost some of their flavor.

For extra color...

... add fresh cilantro

Sweet and sour pork

This delicious Chinese classic offers an exotic combination of very different flavors—sweet pineapple and sour vinegar.

You will need:

1 egg yolk
1½ tbsp corn starch
pinch of salt
1 tbsp milk
8 oz (250 g) lean pork, cubed
2 tbsp canola oil

For the sauce
1 red onion
½ small red bell pepper
½ small yellow bell pepper
1 tbsp canola oil
¼ tsp grated ginger
½ cup chicken broth
1 tbsp soy sauce
½ tbsp light brown sugar
1 tbsp balsamic vinegar
1 tsp tomato paste
8 oz (227 g) can pineapple chunks
1 tbsp corn starch mixed with
1 tbsp water

1 To make the sauce, first chop the onion roughly. Then chop the red and yellow bell peppers into squares.

Scallion curls
I've decorated this dish with scallion curls. To make them, cut a scallion lengthwise into thin shreds, soak in ice water, and watch them curl!

Stir-fry

2 Heat the oil in a wok or a large frying pan over medium-high heat. Stir-fry the onion and bell peppers for 4 minutes, or until they begin to soften.

3 Add the ginger and cook for 1 minute, then add the broth, soy sauce, sugar, vinegar, tomato paste, and canned pineapple with its juice.

TRY THIS WITH CHICKEN
This recipe works well with chicken, too. Simply swap the pork for 2 sliced chicken breasts.

4 Bring to a boil and simmer for 1 minute, then add the corn starch mixture, and simmer for another 2 to 3 minutes, stirring until thickened. Keep the sauce warm over very low heat while you cook the pork.

5 Whisk the egg yolk, corn starch, salt, and milk together. Add the pork and mix until covered.

6 Heat the canola oil and fry the pork over medium heat for 3 to 4 minutes, until it's golden on the outside and cooked completely through. You may need to cook the pork in batches so you don't overcrowd the pan.

Mix the cooked pork with the sauce and serve with scallion curls

Swedish meatballs

You will need:

1 medium onion
1 small clove garlic
3 tbsp canola oil
1 apple
4 slices bread, crusts removed
¼ cup grated Parmesan cheese
1 egg yolk
8 oz (250 g) ground pork or chicken
1 tsp chopped parsley
2 tsp Worcestershire sauce
1 tbsp tomato paste
1 tbsp honey
¼ tsp grated nutmeg
salt and pepper
flour, for dusting

For the sauce

2 tbsp butter
2 tbsp flour
1¾ cups chicken broth
½ cup heavy cream
2 tsp soy sauce
1 tsp Worcestershire sauce

For this traditional dish, I like to use pork because it has lots of flavor. But pork can be fatty, so you might like to try chicken instead.

1 Chop the onion finely and crush the garlic. Heat 1 tbsp of the oil and sauté the onion until it's soft. Add the garlic and sauté for another minute. Cool slightly.

2 Peel the apple and grate the flesh (not the core) into a large mixing bowl. Be careful not to grate your fingers, too!

3 Tear the bread into small pieces (or use bread crumbs) and add it to the bowl. Leave the bread and the apple to stand for 5 minutes.

4 Now add the Parmesan, egg yolk, ground pork or chicken, sautéed onion and garlic, parsley, Worcestershire sauce, tomato paste, honey, and nutmeg.

5 Season with a little salt and pepper, then use your hands to mix everything together thoroughly.

6 Scoop up the meat mixture with a teaspoon and roll it into meatballs. Dust them with flour.

7 Heat the remaining oil in a nonstick frying pan over medium-high heat and brown the meatballs in batches for 2 to 3 minutes, turning regularly. Drain on paper towels.

8 For the sauce, melt the butter and stir in the flour. Remove from the heat and whisk in the broth, a little at a time. Then add the cream, soy sauce, and Worcestershire sauce. Return to the heat and bring to a boil, stirring constantly. Add the meatballs.

To serve
This meal is rich and filling, so you'll only need small portions. Serve it with green vegetables, such as green beans or broccoli, plus plain boiled rice or noodles.

Cook the dish for 5 to 10 minutes before serving

You will need:

2 tbsp flour
salt and pepper
1 lb (450 g) diced lamb shoulder
or leg
2 to 3 tbsp canola oil
1 onion, chopped
1 clove garlic, crushed
½ tsp cinnamon
½ tsp cumin
2 tsp mild curry powder
1¼ cups vegetable broth
1 x 14 oz (400 g) can diced tomatoes
3 tbsp tomato paste
1 tsp honey
½ apple, grated
½ cup dried apricots, quartered

Lamb tagine

Try my special version of a traditional Moroccan recipe. It's meaty, spicy, and fruity all at once!

☆ Annabel's Tip
This dish freezes well, so make twice the amount you need and freeze some for another day.

1 Mix the flour with ¼ tsp salt and a grinding of black pepper. Toss the lamb in the seasoned flour to coat it.

2 Heat 1 tbsp of the oil and brown the lamb—you may need to do this in batches. Put the browned lamb aside.

Serve with rice or couscous, and garnish with fresh cilantro leaves

3 Heat 1 tbsp oil in a deep Dutch oven over medium heat. Add the onion and cook gently for 8 to 10 minutes, until it looks slightly clear. Stir in the garlic, cinnamon, cumin, and curry powder and cook for 2 minutes.

4 Stir in the vegetable broth, a little at a time, then add the canned tomatoes, tomato paste, honey, and grated apple. Stir everything together.

5 Add the browned lamb to the pan. Bring to a boil, then reduce the heat to low. Cover the pan and cook very gently for 1½ to 2 hours, stirring every 20 minutes.

6 Uncover the pan, stir in the apricots, and simmer for another 30 minutes. Add up to ¼ cup extra water if the sauce gets too thick. Add salt and pepper to taste.

You will need:

1 red onion
1 tbsp olive oil
¼ cup light brown sugar
1 tbsp balsamic vinegar
4 sprigs thyme
7 oz (200 g) lean ground beef
1 cup fresh bread crumbs
1 egg yolk
2 tbsp milk
1 tsp soy sauce
salt and pepper
canola oil, for frying

Best burgers

These juicy burgers are made from lean ground beef flavored with caramelized onion, thyme, and soy sauce. They're delicious fried in a little oil, but if you want to cut down on fat, try broiling them instead.

Chop

1 First peel and chop the onion into small pieces. Heat the oil in a nonstick frying pan over medium–low heat. Cook the onion for 8 minutes, or until it's soft. Stir in the sugar and balsamic vinegar.

2 Turn up the heat and cook, stirring, for 2 minutes, until the onion caramelizes (the sugar on it turns light brown). Stir in the thyme. Then transfer the mixture to a bowl and leave to cool.

3 Add the beef, bread crumbs, egg yolk, milk, soy sauce, salt, and pepper. Mix everything together lightly so the burgers stay soft and moist when they cook.

Flatten

4 Divide the beef mixture into four servings. Roll each one into a ball, then flatten slightly into a burger shape. Cover and chill in the fridge.

5 Oil a frying pan lightly, and cook the burgers over low heat for 4 to 5 minutes on each side. Alternatively, broil the burgers for about 4 minutes on each side.

Put your burger in a bun

Bun top

Sliced onion

Tomato

Burger

Lettuce

Mayonnaise

Bun bottom

Do you like cheese?

For a cheesy surprise, put a small cube of Cheddar into the middle of each burger when you shape it. This will give a melted-cheese center.

Chicken burger

You will need:

1 tbsp light olive oil
¼ cup diced onion
1 small clove garlic, chopped
8 oz (250 g) ground chicken or turkey
¼ cup fresh bread crumbs
4 fresh sage leaves, chopped
¼ cup grated apple
salt and pepper
canola oil, for greasing

1 Preheat the oven to 400°F (200°C). Heat the olive oil in a pan and sauté the onion and garlic for about 2 minutes. Allow to cool.

2 Mix the chicken (or turkey,) bread crumbs, sage, apple, salt, and pepper with the cooled onion and garlic. Shape into 4 burgers.

3 Heat a little oil over high heat and cook the burgers for 2 minutes each side. Put them on a baking sheet and bake them in the oven for 10 minutes, or until completely cooked through. ⚠

Fish parcels with tomato sauce

Wouldn't you love to open a steaming parcel for supper? Cooking fish in parchment paper is a delicious way to seal in its goodness.

You will need:

oil, for greasing
2 skinless, boneless, thick white fish fillets (try cod, mahi mahi, or haddock)
salt and pepper

For the tomato sauce

1 tbsp butter
1 small shallot, finely chopped
4 tomatoes, skinned and chopped
2 tsp tomato paste
2 tbsp fish or vegetable broth
½ tsp lemon juice
pinch of sugar
4 basil leaves, shredded
black olives, sliced

1 Preheat the oven to 400°F (200°C). Grease 2 squares (about 12 in/30 cm) of aluminium foil or parchment paper. Place the fish on the foil and season with salt and pepper.

2 Spoon the tomato sauce over the top and wrap up like a package, folding over the edges to seal them.

Fold up

3 Put the parcel on a baking sheet and bake for 12 to 14 minutes, until the fish is cooked through.

To make the tomato sauce, melt the butter and sauté the shallot for 4 minutes, until soft. Add the tomatoes, tomato paste, broth, and lemon juice. Simmer for 3 minutes until thickened. Stir in the sugar, basil, olives, salt, and pepper. Leave to cool.

Salmon...   in a parcel

This recipe
is quick, easy,
and healthy—
and there are
no fishy smells!

Lemon

Lime

Dill

1 Preheat the oven to 400°F (200°C).
Grease a piece of aluminium foil or
parchment paper. Put a salmon fillet, salt and
pepper, dill, and lemon and lime slices on top.

2 Wrap it all up, put it on a baking
sheet, and cook for 15 minutes.

From this...

Wrap the fish in a **parcel**, put it in the oven—and then just wait!

To this

☆ **Annabel's Tip**
*Make sure you seal
your parcel tightly—
if there's a hole where
steam can escape, your
fish may dry out.*

*Simply unwrap and serve with
your favorite vegetables*

Fish bites

I've made these tasty mini mouthfuls with cod, but any firm-fleshed fish will work— why not try mahi mahi or salmon?

You will need:

10 oz (300 g) skinless, boneless fish
2 tbsp flour
salt and pepper
2 eggs, beaten
¾ cup dried bread crumbs
¾ cup grated Parmesan cheese
1 tsp paprika
2 or 3 tbsp canola oil

1 Cut the fish into bite-sized pieces.

Cut

2 Put the other ingredients in separate bowls—flour, salt, and pepper in one, eggs in another, and bread crumbs, Parmesan cheese, and paprika in another.

Put flour, salt, and pepper in one bowl...

Dip

3 Now dip each piece of fish in the flour, then the egg, then the bread crumb mix.

...beaten eggs

☆ Annabel's Tip

To make a slightly crunchier coating for your bites, dip them in a mixture of half bread crumbs and half crushed cornflakes.

4 For an extra crispy coating, dip the fish twice in the egg and bread crumbs.

...and here are bread crumbs, cheese, and paprika

Dip

go in here...

Dip

5 Heat the oil over medium heat— it's ready if it sizzles when you drop in a few bread crumbs. Fry the fish bites for 5 minutes, or until they're cooked through, turning them regularly. Drain on paper towels before serving.

Delicious crispy, crunchy little *nuggets of fish* ready in minutes!

✰ **Annabel's Tip**
Serve with a simple tartar sauce made with 2 tbsp mayonnaise, 2 chopped gherkins, 1 tsp capers (optional), and 1 tsp snipped chives.

Salmon in pastry

These little salmon pastries make perfect picnic food. I've shaped mine into pastry fish, but simple rectangles are lovely, too.

You will need:

3 packed cups baby spinach
1 tbsp butter
1 large shallot or 1 small onion, diced
½ cup ricotta cheese
¼ cup grated Parmesan cheese
pinch of grated nutmeg
salt and pepper
2 sheets frozen puff pastry, thawed to package instructions
10 oz (300 g) salmon fillet, divided into 4 equal portions
1 egg, beaten

SALMON

You will need skinless, boneless salmon for this dish.

1 First, cook the spinach in 1 tbsp water for 2 minutes. Stir and cook for another 2 minutes until wilted. Drain in a colander and leave to cool.

2 Melt the butter in a pan over medium heat and sauté the shallot or onion for 8 to 10 minutes, until softened. Transfer to a bowl to cool.

3 Use your hands to squeeze the moisture from the spinach. Then chop it and add it to the onion along with the ricotta, Parmesan, and nutmeg. Season the mixture with salt and pepper.

4 Cut each sheet of pastry in half. Even though it is ready rolled, it still needs to be thinner, so roll each piece into a rectangle about 6 x 16 in (16 x 40 cm). Divide each rolled-out piece half to give 8 smaller rectangles about 6 x 8 in (16 x 20 cm).

Drape

5 Place a portion of salmon on one piece of rolled pastry, season with salt and pepper, and top with a quarter of the spinach and ricotta mixture. Brush a little beaten egg around the edge of the salmon.

6 Then carefully drape the second piece of pastry over the salmon (or fold over a larger piece) and press down firmly to seal the edges. Trim to make a fish shape.

From this…

… to this!

7 Decorate your fish shape with scraps of cut-off pastry. Brush with beaten egg. Chill for 1 hour. Then preheat the oven to 400°F (200°C). Brush with more beaten egg and bake on a nonstick baking sheet for 25 minutes until golden and cooked through.

Pizza Margherita

Plain cheese-and-tomato (Margherita) pizza is hard to beat. It's totally yummy just as it is, but you might want to experiment with a few of your own toppings...

1 For the dough, use my bread recipe on page 42, but replace the butter with 2 tbsp oil. After the first prove, punch down the dough and divide it into 4 pieces for large pizzas, or 8 for small ones.

2 Preheat oven to 425°F (220°C). Oil a couple of large baking sheets. Roll out the dough into circles, then place them on the baking sheets.

You will need:

bread dough (page 42)
oil, for greasing
tomato sauce (page 82)
8 oz (250 g) mozzarella
cheese, sliced
16 cherry tomatoes

3 Spread a thin layer of tomato sauce on each pizza. Top with mozzarella cheese and halved cherry tomatoes. (Or try a mix of cheeses such as mozzarella with grated Cheddar or Parmesan.) Bake in the oven for 10 to 12 minutes.

Scatter fresh basil leaves over your baked pizza

Season with freshly ground black pepper

Homemade pasta

For this recipe I've used "00" flour, but if you can't find it use bread flour—the pasta won't be as smooth, but will still taste good.

1³/₄ cups "OO" flour
plus extra for dusting

2 eggs

Made by hand
You can make the pasta by hand or in a food processor. And it can be rolled out by hand or using a pasta machine.

2 tsp olive oil

¹/₂ tsp salt

Well

Stir

1 Whisk together the eggs and oil. Put the flour on a work surface and make a well in the center. Carefully pour the egg mixture into the well.

2 Gently stir the flour into the egg, bringing in a little flour at a time.

Keep mixing to make a smooth dough

3 Gradually work more flour into the egg mixture.
Keep going until all the flour is combined.

Mix

Kneaded dough

4 If you want to, mix the eggs and flour using your fingers. Roll the dough into a ball.

5 Put the dough on a clean surface and knead for 5 minutes, or until it feels smooth and silky.

6 Wrap the kneaded dough in plastic wrap and put in the refrigerator to rest for 30 minutes.

1 Cut the dough into four. Roll one piece at a time, keeping the rest of the dough wrapped in plastic wrap.

2 Roll the dough into a rough rectangle approximately 3 x 4 in (7 x 10 cm).

3 Set the rollers of a pasta machine on the widest setting and roll the dough through.

4 Fold the dough into a rectangle and roll again. Reduce the rollers by one notch and roll through again. Keep reducing the width of the rollers until you reach the right thickness.

5 It is best to roll the dough twice through each width (except for the narrowest one). If the pasta gets too long to handle, cut it in half crosswise.

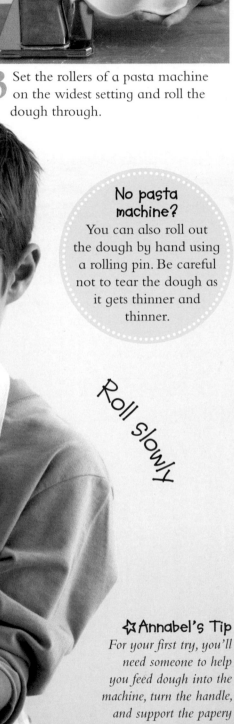

No pasta machine?
You can also roll out the dough by hand using a rolling pin. Be careful not to tear the dough as it gets thinner and thinner.

Roll slowly

☆Annabel's Tip
For your first try, you'll need someone to help you feed dough into the machine, turn the handle, and support the papery dough that comes out.

Making tagliatelle

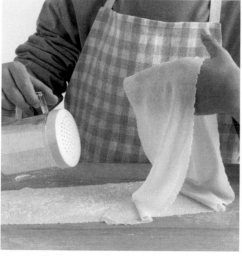

1 Roll the dough through the narrowest setting. Dust it with flour.

2 Fold the dough loosely and cut it into narrow strips.

3 Open out the strips by shaking the pasta gently.

The pasta needs to dry slightly before cooking

Hang it to dry for 15 to 30 minutes

The pasta should feel dry to the touch

You can hang it on a wooden spoon suspended between two candlesticks!

To cook

Bring a large pan of salted water to a boil. Add the pasta and boil for 2 minutes. Drain and toss with one of the pasta sauces on the next page.

Pesto sauce

Adding parsley helps to give pesto its lovely green color. There is enough pesto here for four servings.

Whizz ingredients together

1 First, toast the pine nuts in a dry frying pan until lightly golden. Stir them so they don't burn. Then leave them to cool.

2 Put the Parmesan, garlic, parsley, basil, sugar, and cooled pine nuts into a food processor and whizz until finely chopped. Slowly add the olive oil while the motor is whizzing. Add the water, salt, and pepper.

You will need:

⅓ cup pine nuts
½ cup grated Parmesan cheese, plus extra to serve
1 to 2 cloves garlic
1¾ packed cups fresh parsley
1¾ packed cups fresh basil
pinch of sugar
½ cup olive oil
1 tbsp water
salt and pepper
pasta, to serve

Now use your fresh pesto on a bowl of pasta

3 Cook pasta following the package instructions. Drain and put back into the pan. Add the pesto and toss together. Sprinkle with extra Parmesan to serve.

Tomato and vegetable sauce

You will need:

1 tbsp olive oil
1 red onion, chopped
1 carrot, peeled and grated
½ small leek, thinly sliced
¼ red bell pepper, diced
1 clove garlic, crushed
1 tbsp balsamic vinegar
1 tbsp light brown sugar
1 x 14 oz (400 g) can chopped tomatoes
2 tbsp tomato paste
⅔ cup vegetable broth
salt and pepper

1 Heat the oil in a large pan over medium heat. Sauté the onion, carrot, leek, and bell pepper for 10 minutes, until soft. Add the garlic and cook for one minute, then add the vinegar and sugar and cook for 2 minutes, until the vinegar has evaporated. ⚠️

This makes 4 to 6 servings

2 Stir in the tomatoes, tomato paste, and vegetable broth. Simmer for 25 to 30 minutes until the sauce has thickened. Season with salt and pepper. The sauce can be used as is or pureed for a smoother texture.

Cheese sauce

Serves 4 to 6

You will need:

3 tbsp butter
3 tbsp flour
2 cups milk
½ cup grated Cheddar,
¼ cup grated Parmesan
½ cup grated Gruyère
½ tsp Dijon mustard
¼ cup heavy cream
¼ tsp nutmeg
salt and white pepper

1 Melt the butter and stir in the flour. Turn off the heat and whisk in the milk, a little at a time, to make a smooth sauce. Then cook over medium heat, stirring constantly, until the sauce thickens and bubbles.

2 Then stir in the Cheddar, Parmesan, and Gruyère cheeses, mustard, cream, and nutmeg. Season with salt and pepper (white pepper is nice, since it doesn't show in the sauce).

You will need:

For the roasted vegetables
2 medium zucchini, sliced
2 red bell peppers, cut into squares
1 large red onion, cut into chunks
2 tbsp olive oil
salt and pepper

For the tomato sauce
1 tbsp olive oil
1 large onion, chopped
½ leek, thinly sliced
1 medium carrot, grated
1 celery stalk, thinly sliced
1 clove garlic, crushed
2 x 14 oz (400 g) cans chopped
tomatoes
2 tsp balsamic vinegar
1 tbsp sugar
2 tbsp tomato ketchup
2 tbsp tomato paste
salt and pepper

For the cheese sauce
3 tbsp butter
3 tbsp flour
2 cups milk
½ cup grated Cheddar cheese
½ cup grated Gruyère cheese
pinch nutmeg
¼ tsp Dijon mustard
¼ cup mascarpone cheese or
crème fraiche
¼ cup grated Parmesan cheese
salt and pepper

To put it together
olive oil, for greasing
8 to 9 cooked lasagne noodles
⅓ cup grated Parmesan cheese

☆Annabel's Tip
When you make this lasagne,
cut your vegetables to roughly
the same thickness so they all
cook through correctly.

Vegetable lasagne

This dish is packed with vegetables—chunky roasted ones you can see, and finely blended ones in the sauce. Serve it with crusty bread.

1 Preheat the oven to 400°F (200°C). To roast the vegetables, put the zucchini, peppers, onion, olive oil, salt, and pepper in a baking dish. Gently mix everything together.

2 Cover with foil and roast for 30 minutes. Uncover and roast another 20 minutes, until the vegetables are soft and browning at the edges. Remove from the oven and cool slightly.

3 To make the tomato sauce, heat the oil over medium heat and sauté the onion, leek, carrot, and celery until soft. Add the garlic and cook for one minute.

4 Now add the canned tomatoes, vinegar, sugar, tomato ketchup, tomato paste, salt, and pepper. Simmer for 30 minutes until thick.

5 Leave the mixture to cool slightly, then blend to a puree using a hand blender or food processor.

6 For the cheese sauce, melt the butter and stir in the flour. Remove from the heat and whisk in the milk, a little at a time, to avoid lumps.

7 Put the pan over medium heat and cook, stirring, until the sauce thickens. Take off the heat and stir in the Cheddar and Gruyère so they melt. Then stir in the nutmeg, mustard, mascarpone, and Parmesan. Season with salt and pepper.

PUTTING IT ALL TOGETHER
Oil a baking dish. Put a third of the cheese sauce in the bottom. Then add:

lasagne noodles (1 layer)

roasted vegetables (half)

tomato sauce (half)

You need a rectangular baking dish about 7 x 9 in (18 x 23 cm) and 3 in (7 cm) deep.

Repeat this layering, finishing with the cheese sauce. Then sprinkle the grated Parmesan over the top.

Put the dish on a baking sheet and bake for 35 to 40 minutes

Risotto primavera

This Italian classic is a super-tasty, meat-free, meal-in-a-bowl. It's made with meltingly soft rice, summer vegetables, and Parmesan cheese.

You will need:

1 small carrot
1 small leek
1 small onion
1 small garlic clove
½ medium zucchini
1 tbsp butter

1 tbsp olive oil
1¼ cups risotto rice
5 cups hot vegetable broth
¾ cup frozen peas
½ cup grated Parmesan cheese, plus extra to serve
freshly ground black pepper

Scatter cheese shavings on top before serving

☆ **Annabel's Tip**

For perfect risotto, the rice should be al dente. This means soft but not mushy—when you bite in, it should still be a little firm.

Slice

1 Dice the carrot, then thinly slice the leek and the onion, crush the garlic, and dice the zucchini.

2 Melt the butter in a large saucepan over medium heat. Add the oil, then sauté the onion for 4 to 5 minutes, until it's soft and translucent. Add the leek, carrot, and garlic and sauté for another 2 to 3 minutes until the leek has softened.

3 Stir in the rice and cook for 1 minute, then stir in a ladleful of broth and cook slowly until the liquid is absorbed, stirring all the time.

4 Add the rest of the broth a ladleful at a time—wait until it is absorbed before adding more. Stir the rice regularly during cooking. After about 18 minutes it will be almost cooked through.

5 Add the diced zucchini and peas, plus more broth if necessary. Cook for another 4 minutes, or until the vegetables are cooked through. Remove from the heat and stir in the cheese. Season with pepper, then serve.

Veggie fajitas

I've filled my Mexican-style tortillas with colorful vegetables in a mildly spicy sauce. These are a bit messy to eat—but they're worth it!

You will need:

4 flour tortillas (about 7 in/18 cm)
½ cup grated Cheddar cheese

For the salsa

2 tomatoes, diced
2 scallions, finely sliced
2 tsp lemon juice
1 tsp olive oil
¼ red chile, seeded and diced
       1 tbsp chopped cilantro

For the filling

1 medium red onion
½ red bell pepper
½ yellow bell pepper
½ orange bell pepper
1 tbsp canola oil
⅛ tsp cumin
pinch of paprika
1 tbsp balsamic vinegar
2 tsp light brown sugar
salt and pepper

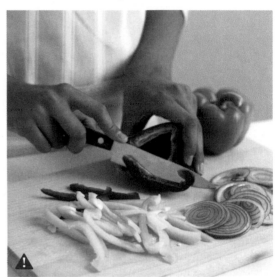

1 To make the salsa, simply mix the ingredients together in a bowl.

2 For the filling, thinly slice the onion. Seed and thinly slice the bell peppers.

3 Heat the oil in a wok or large frying pan and stir-fry the onion and bell peppers for about 4 minutes, until soft. Add the cumin and paprika and cook for 1 minute, then stir in the balsamic vinegar and boil until evaporated. Stir in the sugar and season with salt and pepper.

4 Warm the tortillas in a microwave or dry frying pan, then divide the fillings among them.

☆**Annabel's Tip**
Try adding sliced avocado to your fajita. Avocados are packed with essential vitamins and minerals.

Serve with
sour cream

Start with the onion and bell peppers...

...then spoon over the salsa.

Next, scatter grated cheese on top...

...and finally, roll up your tortilla!

Sweet treats

Learn how to make delicious treats for the whole family to enjoy. Follow my simple instructions and you'll be able to make perfect muffins, cupcakes, cookies, and fruit tarts. Why not organize a cookie and cupcake exchange where everyone brings their own favorite recipe and ingredients and you all learn how to make the recipes and share the treats to take home? Baking has never been so easy or so much fun...

Best muffins ever

Here are five kinds of yummy muffin—the step-by-step pictures show how to make plain ones, and fancy ones are on the next page.

You will need:

1¼ cups all-purpose flour
1 tsp baking powder
⅛ tsp baking soda
¼ tsp salt
⅓ cup superfine sugar
¾ stick butter, melted and cooled slightly
1 egg
¼ cup milk
1 tsp vanilla extract
3 tbsp plain yogurt

1 Preheat the oven to 350°F (180°C). Line a muffin pan with paper baking cups.

2 Put the flour, baking powder, baking soda, salt, and sugar in a large bowl. Mix them together.

3 In another bowl, put the butter, egg, milk, vanilla, and yogurt, and whisk them together.

4 Pour the whisked butter mixture onto the flour mixture.

5 Stir everything together. Be careful not to overmix—the batter should still be slightly lumpy.

SPICY APPLE AND RAISIN
Add 1½ tsp ground cinnamon, ⅓ cup raisins, and ½ peeled, chopped apple to the flour.

ORANGE AND CRANBERRY
Add ⅓ cup dried cranberries and the zest of 1 orange to the flour. Replace the milk with ¼ cup orange juice.

DOUBLE CHOCOLATE
Replace 2 tbsp flour with 2 tbsp cocoa powder. Replace the superfine sugar with ½ packed cup brown sugar. Add ⅓ cup chocolate chips to the flour. Increase the milk to 5 tbsp.

6 Spoon the mixture into the baking cups. Bake for 18 to 20 minutes, until risen and firm to the touch. Cool for 5 minutes in the pan, then remove and put on a wire rack to cool completely.

☆**Don't forget...**
... to add the extra ingredients for these flavored muffins at step 2 in the instructions.

Spicy apple and raisin

Orange and cranberry

Lemon and blueberry

Double chocolate

LEMON AND BLUEBERRY
Add ⅔ cup blueberries and the grated zest of 1 lemon to the flour. Top each muffin with ¼ tsp turbinado sugar before baking.

My favorite carrot cake...

You will need:

For the cake

3 large carrots (about 10 oz/300 g), peeled

1 cup superfine sugar

1⅔ cups all-purpose flour

¼ tsp salt

2 tsp baking powder

¼ tsp baking soda

2 tsp pumpkin pie spice (or 1 tsp ground ginger and 1 tsp cinnamon)

⅔ cup raisins

½ cup sunflower oil, plus extra for greasing

3 large eggs

1 tsp vanilla extract

For the frosting

½ stick butter, softened

1 cup mascarpone or cream cheese

1 cup confectioner's sugar

3 to 4 drops vanilla extract

... and it really *is* my favorite because of its subtle spicy flavor. The carrots in this recipe are what make it scrumptiously moist and sweet.

1 Preheat the oven to 350°F (180°C). Grease an 8 in (20 cm) round cake pan and line the base with baking parchment. Grate the carrots.

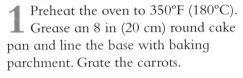

2 Put the grated carrot in a bowl. Add the sugar, flour, salt, baking powder, baking soda, and spice.

Mix

3 Then add the raisins and mix everything together...

Pour

When the cake is cool…

…spread the frosting over the top using a spatula

… as you mix, the juice from the carrots makes the mixture moist and gooey!

☆Annabel's Tip

When your cake is baked, it should be risen and firm to the touch. Push a cake tester into the center—if it comes out clean, the cake is ready.

4 Whisk together the oil, eggs, and vanilla in a pitcher, then pour onto the carrot mixture and stir. Pour into the prepared pan and bake for 40 minutes.

5 **To make the frosting** In a large bowl, mix together the butter and cheese using a wooden spoon. Add the confectioner's sugar and vanilla and stir until smooth.

Decorate with carrots made from rolled fondant icing tinted with food coloring

You will need:

1¾ sticks unsalted butter, plus extra for greasing pan

3 oz (85 g) chocolate

1¼ cups superfine sugar

4 eggs, lightly beaten

1⅔ cups self-rising flour

large pinch of salt

2 tbsp sour cream

1 tsp vanilla extract

1½ tbsp cocoa powder

For the chocolate icing

3 oz (85 g) chocolate

3 tbsp milk

2 tbsp corn syrup

Marble cake

Inside this cake are swirls of chocolate and vanilla. These are made from the same basic mixture, but have different flavorings.

1 Preheat the oven to 350°F (180°C). Lightly grease a 6-cup Bundt pan 8½ in (21½ cm) across and 4 in (10 cm) high.

☆**Annabel's Tip**
You can mix this cake using a wooden spoon. But you might need some help, since it will make your arm ache!

2 Melt the chocolate in a bowl set over a pan of warm water. Then set it aside to cool.

3 Cream the butter and sugar until light and fluffy.

4 Beat in the eggs, a little at a time. If the mixture curdles (separates) add a spoonful of flour and continue beating.

5 Sift the flour and salt together. Fold this into the butter mixture along with the sour cream.

6 Divide the mixture equally between two bowls. Stir the vanilla into one of the bowls of mixture.

7 Add the cocoa powder and chocolate to the other bowl. Stir to combine.

Now spoon your mixtures into the prepared cake pan…

8 Put alternating spoonfuls of chocolate and vanilla in the pan. You can do this in two layers, if you like.

9 Use a wooden spoon to swirl the mixtures into each other for a marble effect. Bake for 50 to 55 minutes, or until the cake is risen and firm to the touch.

To decorate...

... sift a little confectioner's sugar on top

How to make chocolate icing

For the icing put the chocolate, milk, and corn syrup into a heat-proof bowl set over a pan of simmering water. Leave to melt, stirring occasionally. Then cool the icing slightly and drizzle it over the cake.

Alternatively, melt 2 oz (60 g) milk chocolate in a bowl set over a pan of hot water. Leave to cool slightly. Beat ¾ stick softened butter until pale and fluffy. Then beat in ½ cup confectioner's sugar, a little at a time. Stir in the cooled chocolate and spread over the cake.

10 Cool in the pan for 20 minutes. Then turn out onto a cooling rack and leave to cool completely before icing.

☆Annabel's Tip
This cake freezes well. Thaw it out, then ice it just before serving.

... *or drizzle with chocolate icing*

You will need:

- 1 stick butter, softened
- ½ cup superfine sugar
- 1 cup all-purpose flour
- 2 tsp baking powder
- ¼ tsp salt
- 2 medium eggs (at room temperature)
- 1 tsp vanilla extract

Vanilla cupcakes

This is a basic cupcake recipe. You can change the ingredients slightly to make different-flavored cupcakes, or add all kinds of icings and decorations so that each one is a mini masterpiece!

Vanilla cupcakes

1 Preheat the oven to 350°F (180°C). Line a pan with baking cups.

2 Put the butter and sugar in a bowl and beat until pale and fluffy.

Sift

3 Sift the flour, baking powder, and salt onto the butter mixture.

4 Add the eggs and vanilla and beat until just combined.

5 Spoon the mixture into the baking cups. Bake for 18 to 20 minutes, until risen, golden, and firm to the touch.

For chocolate treats... replace ¼ cup of the flour with cocoa.

Add a filling

Cut a cone from the middle of each cupcake. Fill the hole with jam, lemon curd, or icing, and replace the plug. Ice the top with buttercream.

A filled cupcake

Buttercream icing

For plain buttercream, beat 1 stick butter until soft, then beat in 1 cup confectioner's sugar, a tablespoon at a time.

For vanilla buttercream, add ½ tsp vanilla and beat to combine.

For lemon buttercream, beat in 1 tbsp lemon juice—add 1 tsp at a time and taste after each addition.

For chocolate buttercream, beat in ¼ tsp vanilla, 2 oz (60 g) melted and cooled milk chocolate, and 2 tbsp cocoa powder.

Cool cupcakes on a wire rack before decorating

For lemon cupcakes...

... reduce vanilla to ½ tsp and add the finely grated zest of 1 large lemon with the eggs.

Rolled fondant icing

You can buy ready-made rolled fondant icing at cake decorating stores and craft stores. If you want to add color, knead in a few drops of food coloring. Then roll it out and use it to decorate your cupcakes.

Butterfly cake

You'll need about 8 oz (250 g) rolled fondant icing for this. Cut out a set of wings for each cake. Use candies to make each butterfly's body and draw on wing decorations with writing icing.

Chocolate candy

Chocolate monkey

For this, you'll need about 4 oz (110 g) yellow rolled fondant icing. Cut out a yellow circle for each monkey. Cover chocolate cupcakes with chocolate buttercream. Stick on a rolled fondant-icing muzzle, chocolate-wafer ears, chocolate-chip eyes, nose, and hair, and draw on a mouth with icing.

Chocolate chips

Giant chocolate wafer

Cupcake icing ideas

These cupcakes are made using my basic cupcake recipe. It's the icing that makes them special. Swirl it on using a piping bag and tip—but practice on a plate first!

Chocolate curls
To make curls of chocolate you need a bar of chocolate and a vegetable peeler. Then all you do is run the peeler down the back of the chocolate bar. Shake your curls onto a plate and refrigerate until needed.

Decorate with fruit

Chocolate curls

Vanilla

Add pretty sprinkles

For perfect piping, first choose a tip—large ones for thick swirls, and small ones for delicate little blobs and stars. Put the tip in the piping bag, then half-fill the bag with icing. Squeeze the bag from the top as you pipe.

Chocolate cream

Lovely lemon

Caramel

Color your icing

Raspberry and chocolate

Fillings and flavors

Raspberry and chocolate cupcakes
Use vanilla cupcakes. Fill each one with 1 tsp raspberry jam and ice with chocolate buttercream.

Lemon cupcakes
Use lemon cupcakes. Fill with 1 tsp lemon curd and ice with lemon buttercream.

Caramel cupcakes
Use vanilla cupcakes. Fill with 1 tsp caramel sauce and ice with vanilla buttercream. Top with sliced banana.

Chocolate-cream cupcakes
Use chocolate cupcakes. Mix ⅓ cup mascarpone cheese with 2 tbsp cream and ¼ tsp vanilla. Put in the center of each cupcake. Ice with chocolate buttercream.

Chocolate orange brownies

You will need:

- 2 sticks butter
- 7 oz (200 g) semi-sweet chocolate, chopped
- 1½ packed cups light brown sugar
- zest of 1 large orange
- juice of ½ orange
- 4 eggs
- 1 tsp pure vanilla extract
- large pinch of salt
- 1 cup all-purpose flour
- ¼ cup cocoa powder
- 1 tsp baking powder
- ½ cup white chocolate chips or chopped white chocolate

Fudgy or cakelike?

For a fudgy brownie, cook for 30 minutes. (When you push a cake tester into the mixture, soft batter will stick to it.) For a more cakelike brownie, cook for 35 minutes. (Soft crumbs will stick to the cake tester.)

For a special treat, bake a batch of rich brownies. Decide whether you like them fudgy or cakelike, and adjust the cooking time accordingly.

1 Preheat the oven to 350°F (180°C). Line an 8 in (20 cm) square cake pan with baking parchment, making sure the parchment comes up the sides of the pan.

2 Put the butter, semi-sweet chocolate, and sugar in a large heat-proof bowl and set it over (but not in) a saucepan of warm water.

Melt

3 Let the butter and chocolate melt, stirring occasionally. Remove bowl from the saucepan and leave to cool.

4 Prepare the orange zest and juice. Then whisk these together with the eggs, vanilla, and salt until combined.

5 Whisk the egg mixture into the cooled melted chocolate.

Sift

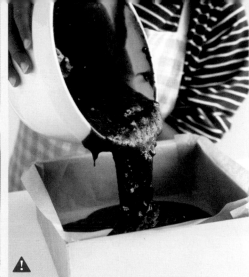

6 Sift the flour, cocoa, and baking powder onto the chocolate mixture and fold it in.

7 Now add the white chocolate chips and fold these in, too.

8 Pour into the prepared pan and bake for 30 to 35 minutes. Let the brownies cool completely in the pan.

To serve, turn the cool brownies out of the pan and cut into squares

Triple chocolate chip cookies

When they're all warm and soft, these cookies are irresistible. They freeze well—if there are any left!

You will need:

1 stick butter, softened
½ packed cup superfine sugar
½ packed cup light brown sugar
1 egg
1 tsp vanilla
1¼ cups all-purpose flour
⅔ cup oats
½ tsp baking powder
¼ tsp salt
2 tbsp each milk, semi-sweet, and white chocolate chips

1 Cream together the butter and sugars until pale and fluffy.

2 Mix together the egg and vanilla and beat into the butter mixture.

3 Add the flour, oats, baking powder, and salt and fold in gently.

4 Then add the chocolate chips and fold them in, too.

5 Line baking sheets with parchment paper. Arrange heaped tablespoons of the mixture about 2 in (5 cm) apart, since the cookies spread during cooking.

Leave space to spread out

ORANGE AND CHOCOLATE
Replace the mixed chocolate chips with ⅓ cup milk chocolate chips and the grated zest of 1 orange.

CHOCOLATE AND CRANBERRIES
Replace the milk and semi-sweet chocolate chips with 2 tbsp white chocolate chips and ½ cup dried cranberries.

CHOCOLATE AND RAISINS
Replace the semi-sweet and white chocolate chips with 2 tbsp milk chocolate chips and ½ cup raisins.

Now chill

6 Chill the cookies in the freezer for 10 to 15 minutes, or in the fridge for 30 minutes. Preheat the oven to 350°F (180°C).

7 Bake for 12 minutes, until golden around the edges. Leave to cool slightly on the baking sheets, then transfer to wire racks to cool completely.

Ginger cookies

These crispy, spicy cookies are easy to cut into exciting novelty shapes, but they're just as nice in plain rounds, squares, or fingers.

You will need:

3⅓ cups all-purpose flour
¾ tsp baking soda
1¼ tsp cinnamon
2¼ tsp ground ginger
½ tsp salt
1½ sticks unsalted butter,
at room temperature
½ packed cup dark brown sugar
1 egg
½ cup molasses

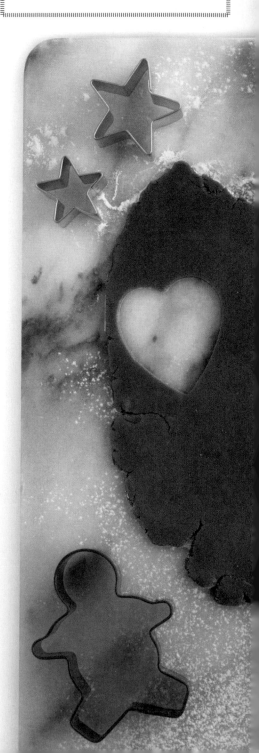

1 Sift the flour, baking soda, cinnamon, ginger, and salt into a bowl and set aside.

2 In another bowl, beat together the butter and sugar until they are light and fluffy.

3 Add the egg and molasses to the butter mixture. Beat thoroughly. (Before you measure the molasses, dip your spoon into oil so it doesn't stick.)

4 Gradually add the flour mixture— just a few tablespoons at a time at first and then in larger amounts. Mix thoroughly.

5 Once the dough is well mixed and smooth, flatten it into 2 round disks about 1 in (2½ cm) thick and wrap them in plastic wrap. Put them in the fridge for at least an hour to firm up.

6 Preheat the oven to 325°F (170°C). Dust a work surface lightly with flour, then roll out each dough disk to a thickness of about ⅛ in (3 mm). Cut shapes out using plain or novelty cookie cutters. ⚠

⚠**7** Line baking sheets with parchment paper and arrange the cookies on them. Bake for 12 to 15 minutes. Let cookies cool slightly on the pan before transferring to racks to cool completely. Try icing with royal icing or writing icing.

You will need:

¾ stick butter
½ packed cup light brown sugar
3 tbsp maple syrup
½ tsp salt
¼ cup chopped dried mango
⅓ cup chopped dried apricot
1 cup oats
1 cup puffed rice cereal
⅓ cup unsweetened, shredded coconut
¼ cup golden raisins

Tropical granola bars

Tuck these sweet, crunchy, high-fiber snacks into your lunchbox, or grab one whenever you need an energy boost. There are two recipes here—both can be stored for up to a week in the refrigerator.

☆Annabel's Tip
Any oats will work in this recipe, but I like the big jumbo oat flakes best, since they give the bars a coarse, chewy texture.

Cool completely *in the pan, then* lift out and cut into bars

Apricot

Golden raisin

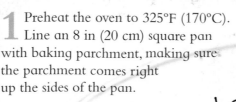

Mmmm—sweet and sticky

1 Preheat the oven to 325°F (170°C). Line an 8 in (20 cm) square pan with baking parchment, making sure the parchment comes right up the sides of the pan.

2 Put the butter, sugar, maple syrup, and salt in a saucepan. Heat gently, stirring occasionally, until it's all melted. Then leave it to cool slightly.

3 Chop the dried mango and apricot into small pieces. Put these in a bowl along with the oats, puffed rice cereal, dried coconut, and golden raisins. Pour the melted butter mixture over the top.

CRANBERRY BAR

¾ stick butter
½ packed cup light brown sugar
3 tbsp maple syrup
½ tsp salt
1¼ cups oats
¼ cup each chopped dried apricots, raisins, dried cranberries, pumpkin seeds
⅓ cup unsweetened, shredded coconut

Put the butter, sugar, and syrup in a large saucepan and heat gently until melted. Remove from the heat and stir in the other ingredients. Then cook as tropical granola bars above.

4 Stir well so the butter and sugar are combined thoroughly with the dry ingredients.

5 Spoon the mixture into the prepared pan and press down well (a potato masher works well for this). Bake for 25–30 minutes until it's golden around the edges.

You will need:

For the pastry

1⅓ cups all-purpose flour, plus extra for dusting

1 tbsp superfine sugar

large pinch salt

1 stick cold butter, cut into small cubes

1 egg yolk, whisked together with 1 tbsp cold water

For the apple filling

2 lbs (900 g) Granny Smith apples

½ cup sugar

½ tsp cinnamon

1 tbsp butter

1 egg, beaten with 1 tbsp water

Homemade apple pie

This traditional dessert is a big favorite in North America—and at my house! I've used sharp green Granny Smith apples here, but sweet eating apples work well, too—just add a little less sugar.

Make the filling

1 For the filling, first peel and core the apples.

Slice

2 Slice the apples into pieces. (Stop them from turning brown by putting them in a bowl of water mixed with 1 tbsp lemon juice.)

Make the pastry

1 Stir together the flour, sugar, and salt in a large bowl. Add the cubes of butter and rub in until the mixture looks like fine bread crumbs.

2 Stir in the egg mixture to make a soft dough. Add extra water, a teaspoon at a time, if necessary. Bring the dough together with your hands. Form into a disk about ½ in (1 cm) thick. Wrap in plastic wrap and chill for 30 minutes.

3 Mix together the sugar and cinnamon. (If you are soaking the apples, drain and pat them dry.)

4 Put half the sliced apples into an oval pie dish about 10 x 7 x 3 in (25 x 18 x 7 cm).

5 Sprinkle half the sugar over the top. Add the rest of the apples, then the remaining sugar. Dot with butter.

Roll

6 Flour a board and rolling pin. Roll out the pastry until it is slightly larger than the dish.

7 Brush the lip of the dish with beaten egg. Lift the pastry on the rolling pin and lay it over the filling.

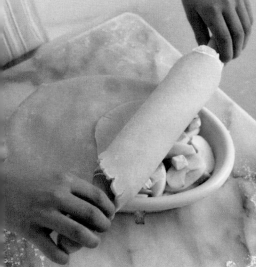

8 Cover the filling completely.

9 Cut away excess pastry with a knife.

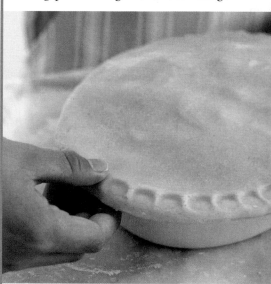

10 Crimp the edge of the pastry to seal it to the dish.

Decorate

11 Decorate with pastry scraps, brush with egg, and cut a steam hole.

Cook on a baking sheet for 20 minutes at 400°F (200°C). Reduce heat to 350°F (180°C) and bake for another 40 minutes.

Delicious served with custard!

Little fruit tarts

These little tarts are made with sweet shortcrust pastry...

Shape

1 To make the pastry, stir together the flour and salt, then rub in the butter until the mixture looks like fine bread crumbs. Stir in the confectioner's sugar.

2 Whisk together the egg yolk, water, and vanilla. Add 2 tbsp to the bowl and mix with a knife. The pastry should stick together. If it doesn't, add more egg mixture 1 tsp at a time. Shape into a ball.

3 Divide the pastry into 8 roughly equal pieces and shape into flat balls. Wrap each piece in plastic wrap. Chill in the fridge for 30 minutes.

7 Take the shells out of the oven ⚠ and leave to cool in the pans for 20 minutes. Then remove from the pans and transfer to a wire rack.

8 For the filling, whisk together the mascarpone, cream or crème fraiche, sugar, and vanilla, until slightly thickened.

9 Spoon the filling into the pastry shells until they are about half full. Top with different types of fresh fruit.

Leave the pastry shells until cold

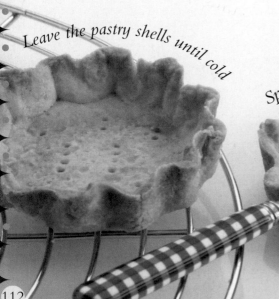

Spread a little creamy filling in the bottom

Top with your favorite fruit...

kiwi fruit and green grapes

You will need:

For the pastry

1⅓ cups all-purpose flour, plus extra for dusting

large pinch of salt

1 stick cold unsalted butter

3 tbsp confectioner's sugar

1 egg yolk

1 tbsp cold water

2 to 3 drops vanilla extract

... and filled with jewel-colored fruits.

Roll

4 Lightly dust a surface and your rolling pin with flour. Then roll out each piece of chilled pastry to around ⅛ in (3 mm) thick. It should be just a little bigger than the tart pan.

5 Use the pastry to line 3 in (7 cm) mini tart pans. Don't worry if you make a hole—simply squash a bit of spare pastry over the gap. Preheat the oven to 350°F (180°C).

6 Trim off the excess pastry. Chill the shells for 10 minutes, then prick the bottoms of the shells with a fork. Put on a baking sheet and bake for 15 to 18 minutes, until golden brown.

For the filling

½ cup mascarpone cheese

½ cup heavy cream or

½ cup crème fraiche

1 tbsp confectioner's sugar

2 to 3 drops vanilla extract

8 oz (250 g) fresh fruit

Dust with confectioner's sugar just before serving

raspberries, strawberries, and red currants

papaya *and* mango

blueberries *and* blackberries

Mini meringues

This recipe comes from Australia, where it's called pavlova, after a Russian ballet dancer. Make four small meringues or one big one.

You will need:

3 egg whites
pinch of salt
¾ cup superfine sugar
½ tsp corn starch
½ tsp lemon juice
⅔ cup heavy cream
6 oz (170 g) mixed berries

1 Cover a baking sheet with parchment paper. Draw 4 guide circles, each about 3 in (7 cm) across. Turn the parchment over—you should still be able to see the circles.

2 To separate the eggs, tip each yolk from one half shell to the other, letting the white fall into a bowl. You only need the whites for this recipe.

3 Preheat the oven to 275°F (140°C). Add a pinch of salt to the egg whites and whisk to stiff peaks. Whisk in 2 tbsp sugar and whisk back to stiff peaks, then whisk in another 2 tbsp sugar and whisk to stiff peaks again.

4 Fold in the remaining sugar, then sift over the corn starch and fold that in, too, along with the lemon juice.

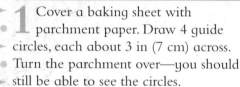

Fold gently

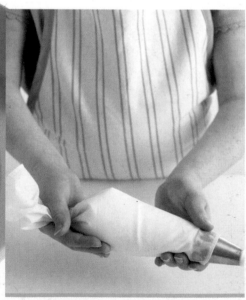

5 Transfer the meringue to a piping bag with a large nozzle.

6 Pipe baskets of meringue on the baking parchment using your circles as guides.

7 Bake the baskets for 1 to 1½ hours, until the meringue is crisp on the outside and pale gold in color. Turn off the oven. Leave the meringues in the oven until they are completely cold, preferably overnight.

☆**Annabel's Tip**

If you don't want to pipe the meringue, spoon it onto the parchment paper and shape it with the back of the spoon.

Whip the cream to soft peaks and spoon on top of the meringue

Decorate with mixed berries

115

Easy berry ice cream

This fresh, fruity ice cream is packed with berries. And you don't need an ice-cream machine to make it!

☆**Annabel's Tip**
If the ice cream is frozen solid, leave it in the fridge for 30 to 40 minutes to soften before serving.

You will need:

1 lb (450 g) strawberries
8 oz (250 g) raspberries
8 oz (250 g) blackberries
1 cup superfine sugar
¾ cup heavy cream
1 to 3 tbsp confectioner's sugar

1 Wash your fruit, pick out any bits of stalk, and hull the strawberries.

2 Put fruit and sugar in a pan, cover, and cook slowly for 5 to 10 minutes.

3 When the berries let out their juice, turn up the heat and simmer for 5 minutes.

4 Let the fruit cool, then blend it until it's smooth.

5 Pour the blended fruit through a strainer to remove the seeds.

6 Pour the strained fruit into ice-cube trays and freeze until solid.

7 Put the cream in a bowl and whip it until it forms soft peaks when you lift the whisk.

8 Let the frozen berries thaw for 5 minutes, then roughly chop in a food processor. Add the cream.

9 Whizz to combine. Add confectioner's sugar to taste. Serve now (it is very soft), or freeze for an hour before serving.

Techniques

Learning basic cooking skills such as chopping, kneading, broiling, and steaming is the first step to becoming a good cook. So here's a simple step-by-step guide that will help you tackle most recipes and turn you into a superstar chef...

Preparing ingredients

After you've read through a recipe and gotten all the ingredients together, the fun can start. First, you need to get everything ready—chop vegetables, grate cheese, prepare bread crumbs, or make stock. Then you can start cooking!

Chopping

Bridge technique
Hold the fruit or vegetable between the thumb and index finger of one hand. Hold the knife in the other hand and cut under the "bridge."

Claw technique
Hold the flat side of the ingredient on the cutting board. Hold your other hand in a claw shape to keep it steady. Move the "claw" along as you cut.

⚠️ Always take extra care when using sharp knives or graters or electrical equipment, including stoves.

Dicing

1 Peel your onion and cut it in half.

2 Cut slices through in one direction, then slice at right angles to the first cuts. Cut across the slices to make cubes.

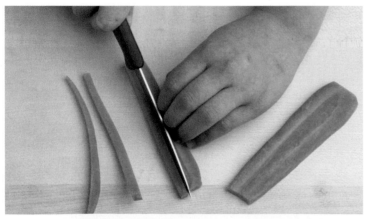

1 Peel your carrot. Then slice in one direction to make "planks." Cut the planks lengthwise to make sticks.

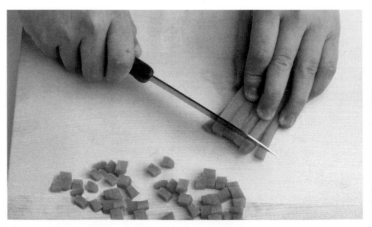

2 Hold the sticks to keep them steady, then cut them into cubes. Try to keep the pieces roughly the same size.

Peeling

Hold a potato in one hand and a vegetable peeler in the other. Run the blade over the potato to peel off the skin. Always peel away from your body.

Use the same peeling technique on a carrot. You might find it easier to peel one end then turn it around and peel the other. Watch your fingers!

To peel a long strip of apple, start at the top and don't lift the peeler off the apple until you reach the bottom.

Grating

Zesting

Hold the grater firmly with one hand. Rub the cheese downward over the teeth of the grater.

Use a grater with small teeth and small holes to grate ginger. Take care—wet foods can be slippery.

The zest of an orange or lemon is just the outside of the skin (not the white pith). Grate this off using a very fine-toothed grater.

Skinning a tomato

The skin slides off easily!

1 First, cut a cross in the skin of the tomato.

2 Cover the tomato with boiling hot water. Leave for about 10 seconds.

3 Drain the tomato and put it in a bowl of cold water. When it's cool enough to handle, peel off the skin.

Making broth

Chicken
Vegetable
Beef
Lamb
Fish

Stir together

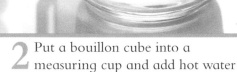

1 There are lots of ways to make broth, but here is how you make it from bouillon cubes.

2 Put a bouillon cube into a measuring cup and add hot water from a tea kettle (see packaging for how much water to use).

3 Stir until the bouillon cube has dissolved. That's it! The broth is now ready.

Making bread crumbs

1 It is easiest to make bread crumbs from bread that is several days old or slightly dried out.

Whizz it up!

2 Tear the bread into small pieces and put it in a food processor. Put on the lid and whizz.

Pour them out

3 In next-to-no-time your bread will turn into bread crumbs. Now they're ready to use.

ALTERNATIVELY

If you don't have a food processor, use a grater instead. Simply rub the bread against the larger holes to make crumbs.

You can also buy ready-made bread crumbs at the supermarket.

Flavoring

You can turn a dull dish into something really special without much effort at all! Here are some easy ways to add extra flavor.

Marinating

1 A marinade adds flavor to ingredients such as chicken. There are many different marinades, so make yours according to the recipe instructions.

2 Then all you do is pour the marinade over the meat. Leave it in the fridge for a few hours or overnight so the flavors can mingle.

When you're marinating meat, make sure it's completely covered. If the marinade is very acidic or salty, don't leave meat in it longer than 20 minutes.

Seasoning

Seasoning means adding salt and pepper to a dish. You don't need much of either—just a pinch of salt and a few grindings of pepper are usually enough.

Preparing garlic

1 Chop off the bottom of each garlic clove. To loosen the peel, crush the clove with the flat side of a knife.

2 To crush it, put the bare clove in a garlic press and squeeze the handles together.

Using herbs

"Soft" herbs such as mint, dill, basil, and parsley can be added at the end of cooking, but "woody" herbs like rosemary, lemongrass, and thyme are best added early on.

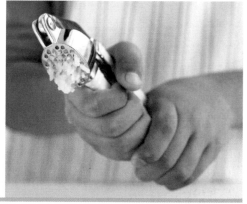

Lemongrass

Dill

Chives

Flat-leaf (or Italian) parsley

Mint

Basil

Cilantro

Curly parsley

Thyme

Baking techniques

Baking is a real treat—I love all the beating, whisking, and kneading it involves, and I love the smell of freshly baked foods. But to be good at baking, you need to know the tricks of the trade. So here they are...

Creaming

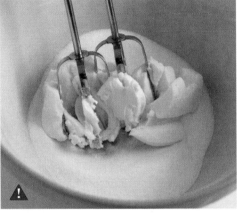

1 When you "cream" butter and sugar, you mix them together. It's easiest to do when the butter is at room temperature and fairly soft. Start by cutting the butter into pieces.

2 Use an electric hand mixer or the back of a wooden spoon to squash and rub the butter into the sugar until everything is thoroughly combined, pale in color, and light and fluffy.

Sifting

This removes lumps and puts air into your mixture. Spoon flour into a strainer, hold over a bowl, and tap the strainer until all the flour falls through the holes.

Folding in

1 This is a gentle way to stir in ingredients without knocking all the air out of a mixture. Use a spatula or metal spoon.

2 Run the spatula around the edge of the bowl, flat against the side. Then draw it across the middle with a cutting action, gently lifting the mixture as you go.

Beating

Hold the bowl in one hand and tip it slightly. Using a wooden spoon, stir the ingredients vigorously to make a smooth mixture and add air.

Separating an egg

1 First, gently tap the egg on the side of a bowl to break the shell. Carefully pull the shell apart.

2 Tip the egg yolk from shell to shell, letting the egg white fall into a bowl. Put the yolk in another bowl.

Whisking egg whites

1 Put your egg whites into a clean bowl—if there is the tiniest bit of grease, the whites won't whisk correctly. To be safe, wipe down bowl and beaters with paper towel dipped in lemon juice.

2 Beat using an electric mixer or hand whisk. The whites will increase in volume as you beat in air. They are ready when they stand in firm peaks.

If you overbeat your egg whites, you will beat out the air and the egg whites will start to collapse.

Preparing a cake pan

1 First, draw around your pan on parchment paper. Cut enough paper to go up the sides of the pan.

2 Spread butter over the inside of the pan so the paper sticks.

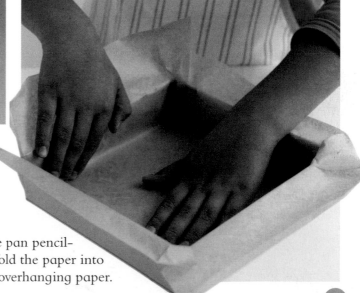

3 Put the paper into the pan pencil-side down. Snip and fold the paper into each corner. Cut off any overhanging paper.

Rubbing in

1 This is a way to mix fat into flour. First, put butter and flour into a bowl. If the butter isn't already cut up, cut the butter into the flour by chopping it into smaller pieces with a knife.

2 Pick up small handfuls with your fingertips. Rub your thumb along your fingertips, letting the ingredients fall. Repeat until the mixture looks like fine bread crumbs.

3 To check that there are no large lumps of butter left, gently shake the bowl from side to side. The lumps will move to the surface and you can rub them in from there.

Kneading

1 This is part of bread making. First, dust a surface with flour. Put your ball of dough on this. Then, use the heel of your hand to squash and push the dough away from you.

2 Fold the top end of the dough toward you. Give the dough a quarter turn.

3 Repeat steps 1 and 2 until the dough is smooth and silky.

Ways of cooking

Recipes use different cooking methods to change the flavor and texture of a dish. Here's a glossary of the ones used in this book.

Boiling

When a liquid is boiling, it is bubbling vigorously.

Simmering

When a liquid is simmering, it is bubbling gently.

Pan frying

When you cook in a pan with a little oil you are pan frying or sautéing.

Stir-frying

Stir-frying is cooking in a frying pan or wok over high heat, stirring constantly.

Broiling

Broiling is a way of cooking food under the heat of a broiler.

Grill cooking

Grill pans heat up on the stove top. Their raised ridges make food look barbecued.

Baking

Baking means to cook food in the oven. Cakes and cookies are baked.

Roasting

When you cook vegetables, meat, or fish in a hot oven, you are roasting them.

Steaming

Steaming is cooking food in a steamer basket over a pan of boiling water.

Index

Annabel Karmel

Annabel Karmel is a best-selling author on cooking for children and her books are published all over the world.

She is an expert in devising tasty and nutritious meals for children without the need to spend hours in the kitchen.

Annabel writes for many newspapers and magazines and appears frequently on radio and TV as one of the UK's experts on children's nutritional needs. She has her own range of healthy foods for children in supermarkets and a co-branded line of children's foods with Disney. She also produces a range of kids' cooking equipment.

Annabel was awarded an MBE in the 2006 Queen's Honours List for her outstanding work in the field of child nutrition.

 annabel karmel

Other children's titles written by Annabel
The Toddler Cookbook   *Cook It Together*
Mom and Me Cookbook

Visit Annabel's website at
www.annabelkarmel.com

Acknowledgments

With thanks from Annabel to: Caroline Stearns, Seiko Hatfield, Dave King, Rachael Foster, Rachael Grady, Mary Ling, Penny Smith, Jonathan Lloyd, Evelyn Etkind, Liz Beckett, **and the children who appeared in the photographs:** Chiara Alongi, Nicolas Alongi, Ruby Christian-Muldoon, Emma Johnson, George Leigh, Fiona Lock, Aliyah Reid, Jordan Robinson, Tom Stewart, and Vikram Garewal.

Picture credits: The publisher would like to thank the following for their kind permission to reproduce their photographs:
Key: a-above; b-below/bottom; c-center; l-left; r-right; t-top)
Alamy Images: Foodfolio 8cr, 127bl; Nic Hamilton Photographic 127c; D. Hurst 8bl.
StockFood.com: K. Arras 79cb; Dave King 127cr; Peter Medilek 57crb.

All other images © Dorling Kindersley
For further information see: www.dkimages.com